Bark + Bite
Culinary Canine Creations for a Happy, Healthy Hound

ISBN Paperback
978-1-989647-39-4

A Byrd Press Publication
Toronto
www.byrdpress.com
publisher@byrdpress.com

cover design and interior art Felipe Silva

For Chester

"The greatness of a nation and its moral progress can be judged by the way its animals are treated." - Mahatma Gandhi

"Dogs are not our whole life, but they make our lives whole."
- Roger Caras

"Tell me what you eat, and I will tell you what you are."
- Anthelme Brillat-Savarin

Bark & Bite

Table of Contents

1

A CASE STUDY: "BEEF BARK AND YAWN" - A SAFE RECIPE FOR DOGS

Welcome, to a culinary adventure that extends beyond the realms of human indulgence - today, we're diving into the world of *haute cuisine* for our four-legged friends. This isn't just about satisfying your taste buds; it's about pampering your pooch with a gastronomic experience fit for the finest furry connoisseurs.

Now, why on earth would we bother with recipes for dogs, you might ask? Well, folks, our relationship with our canine companions has reached unprecedented heights. They're not just pets; they're family. And just as we wouldn't serve rubbish to our family, the same applies to our furry friends. Enter: the world of dog-friendly delights!

Sure, dogs have different dietary needs, but that doesn't mean we can't treat them to some gourmet goodness. It's about understanding their tastes, ensuring their safety, and, most importantly, adding a dash of flair to their food bowls.

So, strap in, my friends, as we embark on this culinary escapade, whipping up a masterpiece that'll have tails wagging in delight. Without further ado, let the feast begin with our Dog-Safe Beef Bourguignon-Inspired Delight. It's not just a treat; it's a canine culinary symphony!

Ingredients

- 1 pound lean stewing beef cut into 2-inch cubes
- 1/2 cup low-sodium beef broth, or our homemade broth
- 1/2 cup dog-safe red wine
- 1/2 cup carrots, chopped
- 1/2 cup green beans, chopped
- 1/2 cup sweet potato, chopped
- 1/2 cup peas
- 1 tablespoon olive oil
- 1 clove garlic, minced
- 1/2 teaspoon dried thyme

Instructions

1. Preheat oven to 350°F.
2. In a large bowl, mix together the beef, beef broth, red wine, carrots, green beans, sweet potato, peas, olive oil, garlic, and thyme.
3. Transfer the mixture to a baking dish and cover with foil.
4. Bake for 2 hours or until the beef is tender and the vegetables are cooked through.
5. Let the mixture cool before serving to your dog.

Note: This recipe is intended as a treat for dogs and should not replace their regular meals. Always consult with your veterinarian before making any changes to your dog's diet.

DOG DELIGHT: A SAFE SLURP AND SNORE

FOLLOWING PROTOCOLS FOR FIDO'S SAFETY

Crafting a dog-friendly rendition of Beef Bourguignon required meticulous consideration of canine health. To ensure our furry friends enjoy a scrumptious treat without any risks, we omitted certain ingredients.

Here's a rundown of what didn't make the cut:

1. Onions: Packed with thiosulphate, a compound that can lead to anemia in dogs when ingested in large quantities.

2. Garlic: Like onions, garlic houses thiosulphate, posing a risk of anemia for dogs in substantial amounts.

3. Bacon: While a human delight, the high fat and salt content in bacon can be detrimental to our canine companions in excess.

4. Red wine marinade: Although red wine is generally safe for dogs in moderation, the typical Beef Bourguignon marinade incorporates onions and garlic, making it a no-go for our four-legged pals. And, when you're on the hunt for a red wine fit for your furry friend, pay close attention. We're not uncorking just any bottle; we're going for dog-safe red wine, and here's the lowdown on what to look for:

First off, no added nasties. That means steer clear of wines playing host to grapes, raisins, onions, or garlic. These are the canine equivalent of kryptonite – toxic, stay away.

Next, moderation is key. Opt for red wines with a touch more class and a bit less kick. High alcohol content? That's a one-way ticket to a not-so-happy doggy stomach. Keep it moderate; they're not running a pub crawl.

Watch out for sneaky sweeteners. Some wines might throw in artificial sweeteners like xylitol, and trust me, that's a big no-no for our four-legged pals. Stick to wines that keep it *au naturel* in the sweetness department.

Lastly, keep it simple. Minimal processing, fewer additives – that's the way to go. We're not in the business of turning our dogs into wine connoisseurs; we're just ensuring they enjoy a safe, uncomplicated sip.

So, there you have it. When it comes to red wine for your dog, it's not just about uncorking a bottle; it's about uncorking the right bottle. Cheers to keeping our furry mates safe and satisfied!

5. Salt: Excessive salt is a canine foe, so opting for low-sodium beef broth and steering clear of additional salt is imperative in our recipe.

In place of these potential hazards, our dog-safe Beef Bourguignon boasts lean stewing beef, low-sodium beef broth, red wine, carrots, green beans, sweet potato, peas, olive oil, garlic, and dried thyme. This carefully curated mix delivers a well-rounded, nutritious meal, supplying dogs with essential proteins, fibers, vitamins, and minerals. We've sidestepped harmful additives such as artificial preservatives and toxins like xylitol and melamine.

Having fine-tuned this recipe, we decided it was high time for a deep dive into the nuances of canine culinary safety.

CANINE CUISINE CAUTIONS: A DOG CHEF'S FIRST LIST OF NO-NOs

Alright, listen up, pet owners. We're diving into the danger zone here, talking about stuff that's as welcome in your dog's diet as a cat in a dog park. Pay attention, because this isn't just a list – it's a survival guide for your furry mate.

1. Onions, garlic, and chives: Forget about Italian night for your pup. These veggies can mess with their guts and wreck those precious red blood cells.

2. Chocolate: No sneaky treats from the candy stash. Chocolate packs a punch with a thing called theobromine, a real deal-breaker for your dog's kidneys.

3. Macadamia nuts: Those fancy nuts are a no-go. Weakness, depression, vomiting – not exactly the perks you want for your dog.

4. Avocado: Guac is off the menu. Avocado has a toxin called persin that can turn your dog's stomach into a war zone.

Avocado-based dog food has become a subject of debate among pet owners and veterinarians. While avocados themselves can be harmful to dogs due to a substance called persin, which may cause gastrointestinal upset, there are dog food brands that incorporate avocado as an ingredient. It's essential to note that these avocados are usually processed and refined for safe consumption by

Several dog food brands use avocados in their formulations, often promoting it as a source of healthy fats, vitamins, and other nutrients. These avocados are typically treated to remove the harmful persin and make them suitable for

canine consumption. These products are specifically designed to be safe and beneficial for dogs.

5. Artificial sweeteners (Xylitol): Keep the sugar substitutes away. Xylitol messes with insulin, and that could lead to some serious low-blood-sugar drama.

6. Grapes and raisins: No fruity snacks for your pooch. These can hit the kidneys like a wrecking ball.

7. Alcohol: No canine cocktail hour. Vomiting, diarrhea, the whole nine yards – alcohol is a party crasher for dogs.

8. Coffee, tea, and other caffeine: Forget about sharing your morning brew. Caffeine can turn your dog into a jittery mess or worse.

9. Milk and dairy: No cheesy surprises. Pets aren't lactose-tolerant, so milk and dairy mean a one-way trip to Upset Tummy Town.

10. Nuts: Keep those trail mix dreams away. Nuts, even the fancy ones, can lead to a vomit fest.

11. Candy (particularly chocolate and any candy containing Xylitol): Double trouble here. Chocolate and Xylitol in candies are a double whammy of toxic nastiness.

12. Potato leaves and stems (green parts): Spuds aren't always buddies. The green parts contain solanine, a real troublemaker.

13. Rhubarb leaves: Leave the rhubarb for pies, not your pup. Oxalates in the leaves are a triple threat to your dog's systems.

And here's the reality check – this list isn't the whole enchilada. There might be other culinary landmines out there, so when in doubt, keep it canine-friendly. Your dog's stomach will thank you. Let's explore...

2 The Essential Background Information Regarding Dog Food

Embarking on a Journey Down the Pet Food Rabbit Hole: Unveiling the Path to Healthy and Safe Choices

Join us as we delve into the intricate world of pet food, unraveling the mysteries of its origins, safety assurances, and the considerations every pet owner should ponder before embracing the commitment to home-cooked meals for their cherished companions.

Exploring the Origins:
First stop – understanding where pet food comes from. Peek behind the curtain to discover the sources of ingredients, the processing methods, and the journey from farm to bowl. Uncover the diversity of choices, from commercial brands to homemade options, each with its unique tale of creation.

Nurturing Health and Safety:
Venture deeper to scrutinize the health and safety aspects of pet food. Unearth the significance of nutritional balance, ingredient quality, and the potential pitfalls lurking in commercial products. Navigate the terrain of regulatory bodies like the FDA, State Departments of Agriculture, AAFCO, and the USDA, each playing a distinct role in ensuring the well-being of our furry friends.

Guardians of Safety:
Meet the guardians standing watch over pet food safety. Understand the responsibilities of regulatory bodies, how they collaborate, and where their oversight extends. Gain insights into the voluntary certification programs, the nuances of inspections, and the delicate dance between federal and state regulations.

Pet Owner's Dilemma:
As we traverse the rabbit hole, confront the crucial considerations facing pet owners contemplating the shift to homemade meals. Ponder the commitment, weigh the nutritional responsibilities, and decipher the challenges involved. Grapple with questions of time, resources, and the delicate balance between ensuring a wholesome diet and meeting the unique needs of individual pets.

In this expedition, we aim to illuminate the path, empowering pet owners with knowledge and considerations to make informed choices. The journey down the rabbit hole is an exploration of the complex and fascinating world of pet food – an odyssey where every decision contributes to the well-being of our beloved companions.

Exploring the Origins: A Glimpse Behind the Curtain

Our journey begins with a quest to unravel the mysteries of pet food origins, inviting you to peer behind the curtain and discover the intricate web that weaves together the sources of ingredients, the processing methods employed, and the fascinating journey from farm to bowl.

Ingredients Unveiled:
Dive into the heart of pet food creation by understanding the origins of its ingredients. Explore the dynamic landscape of protein sources, grains, vegetables, and supplements that form the foundation of your pet's diet. Whether sourced from reputable suppliers or local farms, each ingredient contributes a vital role in crafting a balanced and nutritious meal.

Processing Methods Decoded:
Next on our exploration is a deep dive into the alchemy of processing methods. Uncover the techniques employed to transform raw ingredients into the kibble, cans, or home-cooked delights that grace your pet's dish. From extrusion and baking in commercial production to the careful culinary craft in home kitchens, each method imparts a distinct character to the final product.

In the realm of pet food origins, every choice you make becomes a chapter in the story of your pet's well-being. Our exploration beckons you to be a conscious storyteller, shaping the narrative of your pet's diet with awareness, consideration, and a deep understanding of the journey from farm to bowl.

§

Ingredients Unveiled: Nourishing the Bowl with Nature's Bounty

Our journey into the origins of pet food commences with a spotlight on the elemental building blocks – the ingredients that form the cornerstone of every pet's meal. As we lift the veil on these components, a rich tapestry of diversity and nutritional significance unfolds.

Protein Sources: The Pinnacle of Pet Nutrition

In the grand tapestry of pet nutrition, protein sources emerge as the vibrant threads weaving strength, vitality, and overall well-being for our beloved companions. As we delve into the intricacies of these essential components, the diverse array of protein sources unfolds, each with its unique story and nutritional virtues.

Meats:
The primal essence of pet nutrition often finds its origin in premium meats. Whether it's the succulent goodness of beef, the lean protein of chicken, the omega-3-rich bounty of fish, or the novel proteins like venison or lamb, the journey from pasture to bowl becomes a symphony of flavors and nutrients. The source of these meats, be it from trusted local farms or globally recognized suppliers, plays a pivotal role in ensuring a protein-rich foundation for our pets.

Poultry:
Feathered friends contribute their own chapter to the protein narrative. Poultry, including chicken and turkey, brings not only a lean source of protein but also essential amino acids. The ethical considerations of free-range or organic poultry farming further enhance the appeal of these protein sources.

Fish:
Diving into the aquatic realm, fish emerges as a powerhouse of protein, omega-3 fatty acids, and other vital nutrients. Whether sourced from sustainable fisheries or responsibly farmed, the origins of fish in pet food carry implications for both environmental sustainability and the health benefits bestowed upon our pets.

Plant-Based Proteins:
The rise of plant-based protein alternatives marks a chapter of diversity in pet nutrition. Ingredients like lentils, chickpeas, and peas contribute not only protein but also bring a botanical spectrum of fibers and micronutrients. The sources of these plant-based proteins, whether locally cultivated or part of global agricultural networks, reflect the expanding landscape of nutritional choices.

Novel Proteins:
Venturing into more unconventional realms, novel proteins such as venison, bison, or rabbit add a dash of uniqueness to the protein palette. Sourced from specific animals less commonly found in traditional pet diets, these proteins cater to pets with sensitivities and offer a novel culinary experience.

Ethical and Sustainable Sourcing: Beyond the nutritional aspect, the ethical and sustainable sourcing of protein sources emerges as a crucial consideration. Pet owners increasingly seek assurances of humane practices, responsible farming, and environmental consciousness in the production of the proteins that grace their pet's bowl.

In the world of pet nutrition, where labels provide a snapshot of what's inside the bag or can, delving deeper into the origins of protein sources becomes a mission critical for responsible pet ownership. Here's why understanding the true nature of these sources transcends the glossy promises on the label:

1. Nutritional Transparency:
Labels may offer a generic term like "meat" or "poultry," but the devil lies in the details. Knowing the specific source of protein - whether it's high-quality chicken, grass-fed beef, or sustainably caught fish - unveils the nutritional transparency that ensures your pet gets the optimal balance of amino acids, vitamins, and minerals.

2. Allergies and Sensitivities:
Pets, like humans, can develop allergies or sensitivities to specific proteins. Understanding the precise protein source helps pet owners tailor diets to meet individual needs, avoiding ingredients that may trigger adverse reactions. This level of awareness is especially crucial for pets with known allergies or sensitivities.

3. Ethical Considerations:
For pet owners who prioritize ethical considerations in their purchasing decisions, knowing the protein source's origin is paramount. Were the animals raised in humane conditions? Is the sourcing environmentally sustainable? These questions matter and align with the broader ethos of responsible and compassionate pet care.

4. Quality Assurance:
Not all proteins are created equal. Knowing the origin ensures a level of quality assurance. Was the meat sourced from a reputable farm or supplier? Was it part of a comprehensive quality control process? Understanding the journey of protein from farm to bowl safeguards against potential contaminants and ensures a premium standard of nutrition.

5. Environmental Impact:
The ecological footprint of pet food extends beyond the bowl. Sustainable sourcing of protein contributes to minimizing the environmental impact. Knowledge about whether the fish was responsibly harvested or if the meat comes from a farm with eco-friendly practices allows pet owners to make choices aligned with their environmental values.

6. Variety in Nutritional Profiles:
Different protein sources bring unique nutritional profiles. While some may be rich in certain amino acids, others contribute essential fatty acids or specific vitamins. Understanding this diversity enables pet owners to craft a well-rounded diet that caters to their pet's individual health requirements.

In essence, going beyond the label to unearth the origins of protein sources transforms pet nutrition from a passive act to an empowered choice. It empowers pet owners to make informed decisions that align with their pet's health, preferences, and the broader values they hold dear. The journey from label to origin is a voyage of responsibility, compassion, and the unwavering commitment to providing the best for our cherished companions.

In the grand narrative of protein sources, each option contributes not only to the nutritional symphony but also tells a story – a story of origin, quality, and values. Understanding the intricacies of these protein sources empowers pet owners to make choices aligned with their pet's health, preferences, and the broader ethos of responsible and caring pet care.

Grains and Vegetables: Cultivating Nutritional Diversity for Pets

In the intricate mosaic of pet nutrition, grains and vegetables emerge as the verdant canvas, offering a myriad of nutrients, fibers, and flavors to enhance the well-being of our furry companions. Let's explore the vibrant tapestry of grains and vegetables, understanding their importance and the impact of their origin on the nutritional symphony of pet diets.

1. Carbohydrates and Fibers:
Grains, such as rice, quinoa, and oats, and vegetables like sweet potatoes, provide a wholesome source of carbohydrates for energy. Additionally, their fiber content aids in digestion and promotes gut health. The origins of these grains and vegetables influence their nutrient density and impact on your pet's overall vitality.

2. Essential Vitamins and Minerals:
Vegetables, ranging from leafy greens to colorful bell peppers, contribute an array of essential vitamins and minerals. Whether it's vitamin A for vision, vitamin C for immune support, or various minerals for bone health, the diversity in grains and vegetables ensures a holistic nutritional profile. Understanding their origins adds an extra layer of assurance regarding the quality of these vital nutrients.

3. Antioxidants and Phytonutrients:
The rich hues of vegetables often signal the presence of antioxidants and phytonutrients. These compounds play a pivotal role in combating oxidative stress and promoting cellular health. Knowing where your grains and vegetables come from enhances the appreciation for the antioxidant bounty your pet enjoys.

4. Gluten-Free and Novel Options:
For pets with specific dietary needs, the origins of grains become crucial. Gluten-free alternatives like quinoa or millet cater to pets with sensitivities. Novel grains, sourced responsibly, such as sorghum or amaranth, introduce variety and unique nutritional benefits to the pet's diet.

5. Sourcing from Local Farms:
The concept of farm-to-bowl extends beyond meats to grains and vegetables. Sourcing from local farms not only supports the community but also provides fresher and more environmentally sustainable options. Understanding the farm-to-bowl journey adds a layer of accountability to the origins of these plant-based ingredients.

6. Culinary Variety:
Grains and vegetables contribute not just to nutrition but also to the culinary variety of pet meals. From roasted sweet potatoes to a medley of colorful vegetables, the origins of these ingredients influence the palate, making every meal a gastronomic adventure for your pet.

7. Dietary Customization:
Knowing the origin of grains and vegetables empowers pet owners to customize diets based on individual pet needs. Whether it's choosing low-glycemic options for pets with diabetes or selecting specific vegetables for their unique nutritional benefits, the origin story becomes a guide for dietary customization.

In essence, grains and vegetables are not mere fillers but essential contributors to the nutritional symphony of pet diets. Unveiling their origins adds depth to this symphony, ensuring that every bowl is not just a source of sustenance but a celebration of diversity, health, and the bonds we share with our pets.

Supplements and Additives: Crafting Precision in Pet Nutrition

In the intricate realm of pet nutrition, supplements and additives are the artisans, carefully sculpting the nutritional landscape to meet the unique needs of our cherished companions. These components, though often overlooked, play a pivotal role in enhancing the overall well-being of pets. Let's delve into the significance of supplements and additives, understanding their purpose, and exploring how their origin shapes the nutritional tapestry.

1. Micronutrient Precision:
Supplements come in various forms, delivering essential micronutrients like vitamins and minerals. Whether it's vitamin D for bone health, omega-3 fatty acids for coat luster, or minerals for overall vitality, these micronutrients are the precision tools that fine-tune the nutritional harmony in your pet's diet.

2. Natural vs. Synthetic Sources:
Understanding the origin of these supplements is crucial. Are the vitamins and minerals derived from natural sources or synthesized in a laboratory? The distinction between natural and synthetic sources can impact bioavailability and absorption, influencing the effectiveness of these additives in promoting your pet's health.

3. Joint Health and Mobility:
Supplements like glucosamine and chondroitin sulfate often find their way into pet diets, especially for breeds prone to joint issues. These additives, when sourced responsibly, contribute to maintaining joint health and mobility, ensuring that your pet enjoys an active and comfortable lifestyle.

4. Probiotics and Digestive Health:
Probiotics, considered friendly bacteria, are another category of supplements that support digestive health. Originating from strains like Lactobacillus or Bifidobacterium, these additives aid in maintaining a healthy gut microbiome, promoting optimal digestion and nutrient absorption.

5. Natural Flavor Enhancers:
Additives aren't solely about nutrients; they also include natural flavor enhancers to entice even the pickiest eaters. Understanding the origin of these flavors ensures that your pet's culinary experience is not only enjoyable but also free from artificial additives that may compromise their health.

6. Individualized Dietary Support:
Certain pets may require specialized support due to health conditions. Supplements and additives allow for individualized dietary support, whether it's managing skin allergies, supporting cognitive function, or addressing specific health concerns. Knowing the origin of these targeted supplements ensures that they align with your pet's unique needs.

7. Holistic Wellness:
In the holistic approach to pet wellness, supplements and additives contribute to the overall health narrative. From antioxidant-rich additives for immune support to herbal supplements for calming effects, these components cater to the holistic well-being of pets, addressing not just nutritional needs but also emotional and behavioral aspects.

As we unravel the significance of supplements and additives, it becomes apparent that these components are not mere afterthoughts but integral contributors to the pet nutrition symphony. Knowing their origin empowers pet owners to make informed choices, ensuring that every additive in the bowl is a brushstroke in the masterpiece of their pet's health and happiness.

Local vs. Global Sourcing: Navigating the Crossroads of Pet Nutrition

In the complex journey from farm to bowl, the choice between local and global sourcing emerges as a pivotal crossroads, influencing the quality, sustainability, and ethical considerations of pet nutrition. Let's embark on the exploration of local and global sourcing, understanding the implications and choices pet owners face in crafting the optimal diet for their cherished companions.

1. Proximity and Freshness:
Local Sourcing:
Opting for local ingredients often means proximity to the source. This proximity translates into freshness, with ingredients reaching the manufacturing process sooner. Freshness contributes not only to the nutritional integrity of the ingredients but also aligns with the concept of a more sustainable and community-centric approach.

Global Sourcing:
Global sourcing, on the other hand, may involve a more extended supply chain. While advancements in logistics mitigate delays, the potential for longer transit times may impact the perceived freshness of ingredients. However, it also introduces the prospect of incorporating diverse and exotic ingredients into pet diets.

2. Environmental Impact:
Local Sourcing:
Choosing local ingredients tends to have a lower carbon footprint. The reduced distance for transportation aligns with eco-friendly practices, contributing to sustainability. Supporting local farmers and businesses further strengthens the environmental impact in a positive light.

Global Sourcing:
Global sourcing introduces complexities in terms of environmental impact. While it allows access to a broader range of ingredients, the transportation of these ingredients over long distances may contribute to a higher carbon footprint. Sustainable practices and responsible sourcing become crucial considerations in mitigating these environmental effects.

3. Community Support:
Local Sourcing:
Opting for local sourcing fosters a sense of community support. By choosing ingredients sourced from nearby farms and businesses, pet owners contribute to the local economy. This support extends beyond the pet bowl, creating a symbiotic relationship with the community.

Global Sourcing:
Global sourcing may offer economic opportunities to communities worldwide. While it doesn't provide the same direct community support as local sourcing, it facilitates trade and collaboration on a global scale, potentially uplifting economies in various regions.

4. Transparency and Accountability:
Local Sourcing:
Local sourcing often comes with increased transparency. Knowing the local farmers and suppliers enables a closer understanding of their practices. This transparency fosters accountability, as pet owners can directly inquire about sourcing standards and ethical considerations.

Global Sourcing:
Global sourcing may present challenges in terms of transparency. While reputable brands strive for transparency, the complexity of a global supply chain can create hurdles in tracing the origin of every ingredient. Certifications and partnerships with trusted suppliers become essential in ensuring accountability.

5. Ingredient Diversity:
Local Sourcing:
Local sourcing may limit the availability of certain ingredients, especially those not native to the region. However, it encourages the use of seasonal and locally available ingredients, promoting a diverse yet region-specific approach.

Global Sourcing:
Global sourcing opens the door to a wider array of ingredients from different climates and regions. This diversity allows for more exotic and specialized options, catering to specific nutritional needs and preferences.

6. Cost Considerations:

Local Sourcing:
Local sourcing may be associated with higher costs due to factors such as smaller-scale production and adherence to local regulations. However, pet owners often view these costs as an investment in supporting ethical and sustainable practices.

Global Sourcing:
Global sourcing can sometimes lead to cost efficiencies, especially when dealing with large-scale production and access to ingredients on a global scale. However, this doesn't necessarily guarantee lower costs, as factors like quality and ethical sourcing practices still play a significant role.

In the dynamic landscape of local and global sourcing, pet owners navigate a terrain of choices, each with its set of advantages and considerations. Whether opting for the familiarity of local ingredients or embracing the diversity offered by global sourcing, the decision ultimately rests on aligning with personal values, environmental consciousness, and the well-being of our beloved pets.

Ethical Considerations

Navigating the realm of ethical pet nutrition involves a holistic approach that extends beyond merely meeting dietary requirements. It's a conscious journey guided by compassion and responsibility. When selecting ingredients, prioritize animal welfare by opting for those sourced responsibly, avoiding low-quality by-products that may compromise ethical standards. Embrace sustainability by choosing eco-friendly packaging and considering alternative protein sources, contributing to a reduction in environmental impact.

Opt for transparency in brands, favoring those that openly disclose ingredient sources and adhere to fair labor practices, ensuring ethical treatment of workers in the pet food industry. Beyond the bowl, consider broader issues like pet overpopulation, actively supporting initiatives that promote responsible practices such as spaying/neutering and adoption from shelters. Engage in ongoing education, raising awareness about ethical sourcing, cultural considerations, and sustainability within the pet food industry. In the tapestry of ethical pet nutrition, each choice becomes a brushstroke, painting a portrait of empathy, consciousness, and commitment to the well-being of our cherished animal companions and the world they inhabit.

As we unveil the ingredients, it becomes apparent that each element contributes not just nutrition but also a story – a story of where it comes from, how it was produced, and the values it embodies. In the world of pet food, understanding these origins empowers pet owners to make choices that align with their pet's health and the broader vision of a conscientious and caring approach to pet nutrition.

Processing Methods Decoded

Now, let's have a look at the processing methods in the commercial dog food industry, shall we? On one side of the coin, you've got benefits galore for the business moguls. Extrusion, the golden child of commercial production, ensures efficiency – cranking out kibble at an impressive rate. Baking, another contender, brings that enticing aroma and texture. It's a production-line ballet, creating consistency and shelf-stability for the masses. But, here's the kicker for us, the pet owners. Behind the scenes, there are hazards lurking like gremlins in the dark. The high-heat extravaganza can zap the nutrients from the ingredients, leaving us with a nutritional shell of what could've been. Add preservatives to the mix – those sneaky fellas that keep the food shelf-stable but might play havoc with your pup's well-being. So, as we dive into the smorgasbord of commercial dog food, tread carefully, my friends, for the benefits to business might come at a cost to our four-legged companions.

Extrusion: Unveiling the Double-Edged Sword

Benefits:
Extrusion, the heavyweight in commercial dog food production, brings a plethora of benefits to the table. It's like the superhero of kibble-making, offering efficiency in large-scale production, ensuring uniformity in shape, size, and texture. The high-heat process kills off harmful bacteria, providing a safer product for our furry friends. Shelf-stability is the cherry on top, allowing for longer storage without compromising quality.

Downsides:
Now, let's unmask the potential downsides. The high temperatures during extrusion might be a double-edged sword. While they eliminate harmful bacteria, they can also strip away some of the nutritional goodness from the ingredients. Think of it as a culinary magic trick – some nutrients disappear into the ether. Additionally, the reliance on preservatives to maintain that extended shelf life could raise eyebrows. For pet owners, it's a delicate balance between convenience and ensuring our pets get the best nutritional bang for their buck.

Baking: The Culinary Ballet of Commercial Canine Cuisine

Benefits:
Enter the artisanal touch of baking in commercial dog food. It's like the slow dance of flavors, creating a product with an inviting aroma and palatable texture. Baking, unlike the high-heat extrusion, is a gentler process that retains more of the natural flavors and nutritional goodness of the ingredients. The end result often feels closer to home cooking, appealing to pet owners who want a balance between convenience and quality.

Downsides:
However, this ballet has its pitfalls. While baking retains more nutrients than extrusion, it might not be as efficient for large-scale production. The products also tend to have a shorter shelf life compared to their extruded counterparts. Pet owners seeking the convenience of longer storage might find themselves choosing between durability and the more nuanced flavors retained through baking.

Home Cooking for Your Dog: A Feast of Benefits

1. Tailored Nutrition:
　　Home cooking allows you to tailor your dog's meals to their specific nutritional needs. Whether your pup requires a specialized diet for health conditions or simply has preferences, you have the flexibility to craft meals that cater to their individual requirements.

2. Quality Ingredients:
　　With home cooking, you have control over the quality of ingredients. You can choose fresh, whole foods, ensuring that your dog receives a nutrient-rich and minimally processed diet. This can contribute to overall health and well-being.

3. Variety and Rotation:
　　Dogs, much like humans, benefit from a diverse diet. Home cooking enables you to introduce a variety of proteins, vegetables, and grains, promoting a well-rounded and balanced nutritional intake. Rotation also reduces the risk of developing food sensitivities.

4. Avoidance of Additives:
　　By cooking at home, you can eliminate or control additives and preservatives that are often present in commercial dog food. This can be particularly beneficial for dogs with sensitivities to certain ingredients.

5. Improved Digestibility:
　　Freshly prepared, home-cooked meals can be easier for dogs to digest compared to highly processed commercial options. This is especially advantageous for dogs with digestive issues or sensitive stomachs.

6. Bonding and Engagement:
　　The process of preparing meals for your dog fosters a deeper bond and engagement. It becomes a shared experience, and the act of serving a homemade meal can create a positive association with food, enhancing the overall dining experience for your pup.

7. Monitoring and Adjusting:
　　Home cooking allows you to closely monitor your dog's weight and adjust portion sizes accordingly. This level of control is valuable for managing your dog's weight and preventing obesity or other weight-related issues.

8. Response to Health Conditions:
　　For dogs with specific health conditions, such as allergies or kidney disease, home cooking provides an avenue to address these concerns through carefully curated ingredients and recipes. It allows you to work in conjunction with your veterinarian to create a diet that supports your dog's health.

9. Overall Well-Being:
　　The holistic approach of home cooking contributes to your dog's overall well-being. From the physical benefits of a nutritious diet to the emotional well-being derived from the attention and care involved in the process, home-cooked meals can enhance your **dog's** quality of life.

While the benefits are numerous, it's essential to approach home cooking with the right knowledge. Ensuring that meals are nutritionally complete and balanced requires research or consultation with a veterinarian or canine nutritionist. With the proper guidelines in place, home cooking becomes a rewarding and health-conscious choice for your furry companion.

The Pet Food Balancing Act: Quick Guide for Owners

Convenience vs. Nutrition:
Pet food choices often boil down to convenience versus nutrition. While commercial options offer ease, they may lack the personalized nutrition some dogs need. Home cooking provides customization but demands more time and effort.

Quality Matters:
Prioritize quality over quantity. Commercial foods boast convenience but may hide additives. Home-cooked meals ensure fresh, wholesome ingredients, minimizing risks associated with processing.

Time Factor:
Balancing act tip: Acknowledge the time factor. Home cooking demands more effort, but it allows control over ingredients. For busy owners, finding the right balance is key.

Guidance is Key:
Navigating the realm of dog nutrition becomes a smoother journey with the expert guidance of professionals. These nutritional navigators tailor diets to your dog's uniqueness, addressing specific needs based on breed, age, size, and health conditions. They play a crucial role in spotting and managing allergies and health concerns, ensuring your pup thrives. Offering insights on portion control, they help maintain a healthy weight, a cornerstone of overall well-being. Crafting well-rounded diets, they contribute to vitality and immune health. As your dog's needs evolve, these experts adapt diets, providing ongoing guidance for a lifetime of optimal nutrition. Trust in their expertise – it's the compass leading your furry friend to a healthier and happier life.

Holistic Well-Being:

In the pursuit of holistic well-being, it's essential to extend the same care to both yourself and your beloved pet. For you, it involves maintaining a balanced lifestyle, encompassing physical health, mental well-being, and emotional fulfillment. Regular exercise, a nutritious diet, and moments of relaxation contribute to your overall vitality.

Parallelly, your pet's holistic well-being revolves around similar principles. Ensuring they receive a nutritious diet tailored to their needs, regular veterinary check-ups, and ample physical activity are key components. Emotional enrichment, whether through play, bonding, or mental stimulation, is equally vital for their happiness.

This shared journey towards holistic well-being creates a harmonious and fulfilling life for both you and your pet. The bond you share becomes a source of mutual support, enhancing the joy and longevity you experience together. Remember, as you nurture your well-being, you're also contributing to the vibrant health and happiness of your cherished four-legged companion.

THINGS TO CONSIDER WHEN THINKING ABOUT YOUR DOG'S DIET

1. Life Stage: Consider your dog's life stage—puppy, adult, or senior. Different life stages have varying nutritional needs.

2. Breed and Size: Large and small breeds may have different dietary requirements. Tailor the diet to your dog's specific size and breed characteristics.

3. Activity Level: Active dogs may need more calories and specific nutrients to support their energy levels, while less active dogs may require a more calorie-controlled diet.

4. Health Conditions: If your dog has any health issues or allergies, consult with your veterinarian to determine an appropriate diet that addresses these concerns.

5. Weight Management: Keep an eye on your dog's weight and adjust the portion sizes accordingly. Maintaining a healthy weight is crucial for overall well-being.

6. Dietary Preferences: Some dogs may have preferences for certain flavors or textures. Experiment with different types of food to find what your dog enjoys.

7. Food Allergies: Be aware of any food allergies your dog may have. Common allergens include certain proteins, grains, or additives.

8. Nutritional Balance: Ensure that your dog's diet provides a balanced mix of proteins, fats, carbohydrates, vitamins, and minerals. This balance is crucial for their overall health.

9. Hydration: Make sure your dog has access to fresh water at all times. Proper hydration is essential for digestion and overall well-being.

10. Treats and Snacks: Monitor the intake of treats and snacks. While they can be a part of the diet, excessive treats can lead to weight issues.

11. Consult with a Veterinarian: Regularly consult with your veterinarian to discuss your dog's diet and any necessary adjustments. A vet can provide personalized recommendations based on your dog's health and specific needs.

12. Transitioning Foods: If changing your dog's diet, gradually transition from one food to another over a week to minimize digestive upset.

13. Read Labels: Check the ingredients list on dog food labels. Look for high-quality ingredients and avoid artificial additives.

14. Avoid Harmful Foods: Be aware of foods that are toxic to dogs, such as chocolate, onions, garlic, and certain fruits. Ensure that your dog's diet avoids these harmful substances.

15. Regular Exercise: Combine a balanced diet with regular exercise to maintain your dog's overall health and fitness.

Always consult with your veterinarian before making significant changes to your dog's diet or if you have specific concerns about their health.

Key Considerations in Crafting a Tailored Meal Plan for Your Dog

Alright, let's break this down. When it comes to feeding our four-legged friends, it's not a one-size-fits-all scenario. Sure, dogs have some common nutritional ground, but there's a symphony of factors that can throw in a twist, creating a unique dietary composition for each pup.

First off, take a look at the breed. You've got your giants and your minis, each with their own playbook of nutritional demands. Large breeds, they're like the linebackers; you need to manage their calories carefully to avoid the puppy fat turning into a doggy spare tire. Now, the little guys, they might need more calories per pound – it's like they're running on a high-octane fuel compared to their bigger counterparts.

Size, my friend, is another game-changer. Whether you've got a Great Dane or a Chihuahua, their size plays a role in what goes into the bowl. You wouldn't feed a linebacker the same portions as a gymnast, would you?

Age – that's a critical act in this culinary drama. Puppies, they're like the teenage athletes, needing a diet rich in calories and protein to fuel that rapid growth. Seniors, on the other hand, they might need a more lean and mean diet to avoid packing on the pounds.

Now, let's talk about energy levels. Picture this: you've got a dog that's sprinting around the park like it's on a mission from the doggy gods. That one needs a diet with extra fuel, the kind that powers them through the canine Olympics. On the flip side, a dog that prefers the couch over the track? Well, that's a different menu altogether, my friend – one that's lighter on the calories to keep that waistline in check.

And health conditions – that's the wildcard. Dogs dealing with health issues, be it diabetes or kidney trouble, they need a customized menu to manage their conditions. It's like crafting a special dish for a VIP – attention to detail is key.

So, when I say dogs share general nutritional needs but have unique dietary requirements, I mean it's a culinary journey that requires a bit of finesse. It's not about slapping the same meal in every bowl; it's about understanding the nuances, the individual quirks that make each dog a culinary conundrum. It's a challenge, but trust me, the reward is a tail-wagging, satisfied customer. That's the goal – happy, healthy, and well-fed.

Breed-Specific Dietary Insights

While the majority of our canine companions can thrive on a standard diet, certain breeds demand a more tailored approach when it comes to their nutrition.

Let's break it down:

1. Large Breed Dogs:
- These majestic giants require a diet that's not as heavy on the calories, warding off the twin specters of obesity and joint issues.

2. Small Breed Dogs:
- It's like feeding the little powerhouses. Small breeds often need more calories per pound compared to their larger counterparts to fuel their perpetual energy.

3. Short-Snouted Breeds:
- Bulldogs and pugs, with their distinctive snub noses, might prefer a diet that's easier on their jaws. Think smaller kibble or wet food – something that doesn't feel like tackling a feast.

4. Dalmatians:
- These spotty companions are prone to bladder stones. Cue a diet low in purines to keep those stones at bay and maintain urinary bliss.

5. Golden Retrievers:
- Ah, the lovable Goldens. With their hearts as big as their personalities, they benefit from a diet that supports cardiac health. Keep those ticker troubles at bay.

6. Breeds with Allergies or Sensitivities:
- Some breeds are more prone to food-related dramas. They might need a special diet to navigate the tricky terrain of allergies or sensitivities without any tummy tantrums.

Now, here's the kicker – breed-specific diets exist, but they might not be the silver bullet for every health concern. It's like having a tailored suit – it fits well, but you need to check if it's got all the right pockets. Comparing the nutrient levels to your vet's goals is the key here.

So, while many dogs can share a meal plan, these specific breeds might raise an eyebrow and say, 'Hold on, I need something special.' A bit of expert advice from your vet? That's the secret sauce to a diet that suits your pup like a custom-tailored suit. Always wise to consult with the doggy nutrition maestro – your veterinarian – for the perfect recipe tailored to your furry friend's individual needs.

Unwanted Additions in Commercial Dog Chow

Listen up, pet parents. Not all commercial dog foods are created equal, and some contain ingredients that could turn your pup's mealtime into a health hazard. Let's shine a light on some of these unsavory characters:

1. BHA/BHT:
- Let's unravel the story of BHA/BHT, the preservatives that play a dual role in extending the shelf life while harboring a dark side for our furry companions.

BHA (butylated hydroxyanisole) and BHT (butylated hydroxytoluene) step onto the scene as guardians of freshness, aiming to keep those kibble and treats from turning into a culinary time bomb. The intent is clear – a prolonged shelf life means less waste and more convenience. However, there's a twist in this tale.

These preservatives, while battling the march of time in pet food, have been implicated in health concerns for our four-legged friends. The dark side emerges as studies hint at potential links to health problems, with the ominous shadow of the 'C' word – cancer – looming over the narrative.

It's like a paradoxical dance of preservation and potential peril. On one hand, BHA/BHT strives to maintain the integrity of the food, and on the other, questions arise about the toll it might take on the health of our beloved pets. The notion that these preservatives could be associated with cancer in dogs casts a somber shadow over their seemingly innocuous role.

While regulatory bodies set limits on the allowable levels of BHA/BHT in pet food, debates persist about whether these thresholds truly guarantee long-term safety. It's akin to walking a tightrope, ensuring a delicate balance between food preservation and safeguarding the well-being of our furry companions.

For pet owners navigating the pet food aisles, this revelation might prompt a closer look at alternative options, steering towards products that rely on natural preservatives or those with a cleaner ingredient profile. After all, the health and happiness of our pets deserve a narrative free from shadows and uncertainties.

2. Propylene Glycol:
- Let's spotlight the character known as Propylene Glycol, a substance that makes its way into the pet food plot with a mission to maintain moisture. Here's the lowdown:

Propylene Glycol takes the stage as a humectant, tasked with the responsibility of keeping pet food moist and appetizing. Imagine it as the guardian against dry and lackluster meals, ensuring that every bite is as enjoyable as the first.

However, there's a twist in this moisture-retaining tale. Propylene Glycol, while performing its role as a humectant, has been associated with potential health problems for our four-legged companions. It's like a paradoxical scenario where the quest for palatability might come at a cost.

Reports suggest that Propylene Glycol, in higher quantities, can lead to health issues such as anemia in dogs. It's like a side effect sneaking into the narrative, creating a subplot of concern amid the quest for well-preserved and appealing pet food.

While regulatory bodies set acceptable limits for Propylene Glycol in pet food, questions linger about the long-term impact, especially considering its potential to pose risks at higher concentrations.

For pet owners navigating the world of pet food, this revelation might prompt a more discerning eye when scanning ingredient lists. Opting for products with alternative moisture-retaining methods or natural alternatives ensures that the quest for delicious and hydrating meals doesn't compromise the health and vitality of our beloved pets. After all, a well-hydrated and healthy pet is the true star of this culinary tale.

3. Ethoxyquin:

- Let's take a deeper dive into the enigmatic world of Ethoxyquin, a player in your dog's food that operates like a pesticide with a flair for hide-and-seek.

Picture this: Ethoxyquin steps onto the stage with the role of preserving fats and oils in your pet's food. It's like the guardian of freshness, ensuring those lip-smacking flavors stay intact. However, here's the plot twist – this preservative has been implicated in potential health concerns, particularly for the liver and kidneys.

Imagine your dog's body as a finely tuned instrument, each organ playing a vital note in the symphony of health. Now, Ethoxyquin, while busy warding off the rancidity of fats, may have a darker side. Reports suggest a potential link between this preservative and adverse effects on liver and kidney function in some dogs.

It's like a double-edged sword – on one hand, preserving the food's integrity, and on the other, potentially posing risks to your pup's internal orchestra. The liver, responsible for detoxification and nutrient processing, and the kidneys, crucial for waste elimination, could face a challenging melody with the prolonged presence of Ethoxyquin.

While regulatory bodies have set limits on the amount of Ethoxyquin allowed in pet food, the debate continues on whether these limits truly ensure long-term safety. It's a bit like regulating a dance, ensuring it stays within certain bounds, but questions linger about the lasting impact.

So, when it comes to Ethoxyquin, it's not just a silent player in the background; it's a character with complexities. Pet owners might find solace in exploring pet foods with alternative preservatives or natural preservation methods, ensuring their furry companions enjoy a culinary experience that doesn't compromise their long-term well-being.

4. Artificial Colors and Flavors:

- Appealing to the eyes, maybe, but these additives can trigger allergic reactions and a host of other health concerns.

5. Corn and Soy:

- Corn and soy, common players in pet food, bring both benefits and concerns to the table. Corn serves as an affordable filler, but its digestibility can be challenging, especially in genetically modified forms. Soy, contributing plant-based protein, has its merits, but it's a common allergen for some dogs. For pet owners seeking alternatives, exploring grain-free options or foods with different protein sources ensures a more tailored and easily digestible diet for their furry friends.

6. Meat By-Products:

- Not fit for your dinner table, and definitely not for your dog's. Low-quality animal parts that can play host to harmful bacteria and contaminants.

7. Wheat and Other Grains:

- Allergens in disguise. These can bring on digestive distress and a parade of other health problems for your pup. "Wheat and Other Grains" are often added to dog food for their cost-effectiveness, but they may pose challenges for some pups. Here's the lowdown:

Digestive Woes: Grains, especially wheat, can be tough on some dogs' stomachs, leading to digestive issues. It's like serving up a dish that doesn't agree with everyone at the table.

Allergen Alert: These ingredients are known allergens for certain dogs. Just like humans, some pups might have sensitivities, resulting in allergic reactions and skin problems.

Genetic Modification Risk: Many commercial grains are genetically modified, and the long-term effects of these modifications on canine health are still under scrutiny. It's like introducing an unknown variable to your dog's diet equation.

So, while "Wheat and Other Grains" might bulk up the kibble, they might not be the best fit for every furry friend. Opting for grain-free or limited-ingredient dog food can be a thoughtful choice, ensuring your pup's bowl is filled with ingredients that suit their individual needs. After all, a well-fed dog is a happy dog.

8. "Meat Meal" or "Meat and Bone Meal":
- Sounds hearty, but it's a sneaky source of low-quality protein that might be packing some unwanted guests – harmful chemicals and contaminants. "Meat Meal" typically involves rendering and grinding meat into a concentrated form. Now, the catch here is that it can encompass a variety of meat sources, and the specifics might remain undisclosed. It's a bit like a meat medley where you're not quite sure what's in the mix.

"Meat and Bone Meal" takes it a step further by including ground bones in the mix. While bones can provide some nutritional benefits, the quality can be variable, and there's a risk of contaminants.

So, while these ingredients might sound hearty, they often lack the transparency needed to know exactly what your pet is getting. Opting for dog foods with clearly specified meat sources and high-quality protein is a safer way to ensure your pup gets the nutrition they deserve. After all, clarity in ingredients is key to a well-balanced bowl.

9. "Animal Digest":
- A flavor enhancer that's less gourmet and more risky business. Made from by-products, it can bring along a side of harmful chemicals and contaminants.

The challenge with "Animal Digest" lies in its mystery. The term encompasses a range of animal by-products, and the specific sources might remain undisclosed. It's like a culinary concoction where you're not quite sure about the ingredients used.

Moreover, this flavor enhancer could potentially include parts of animals that may not be fit for human consumption. It's a bit like adding an element of uncertainty to the recipe.

10. "Rendered Fat":
- Let's demystify 'rendered fat.' In commercial dog food, it's not the culinary delight it might sound like. This fat is extracted through a process that can mix various animal tissues, making its origin a bit of a mystery. Plus, during rendering, it can pick up unwanted guests like harmful chemicals and toxins. Nutritionally, it might lack essential elements, leaving your pup with an incomplete meal. When it comes to your dog's diet, opting for fats with a clear nutritional profile is the safer bet. After all, you want your pup's meal to be a delight, not a gamble.

Now, this list isn't exhaustive. There might be other bad actors lurking in commercial dog food. The golden rule? Read those ingredient labels like a detective on a mission. Opt for high-quality dog food that skips the harmful additives and fillers. Your pup's health is worth the extra scrutiny at mealtime.

Navigating the Regulatory Landscape for Commercial Dog Food in the U.S.

When it comes to pet food in the United States, there's a dual regulatory dance conducted by both federal and state authorities. Taking center stage is the Food and Drug Administration (FDA), donning the responsibility cape to ensure that Fido's fare is not just safe but also well-crafted and truthfully labeled.

The FDA approaches the regulation of pet food akin to its oversight of other animal foods. This means there's a checklist: proper product identification, a clear net quantity statement, disclosure of the manufacturer or distributor's name and location, and a transparent list of ingredients, neatly arranged from most to least by weight[3].

But here's where it gets interesting – each state brings its own flair to the regulatory tango. Many states follow labeling guidelines, often mirroring the model laid out by the Association of American Feed Control Officials (AAFCO). It's a bit like having a shared rhythm but with each state adding its unique twist.

However, the plot thickens. While these regulations ensure the safety and identification of ingredients, they may not always cater to the specific nutritional needs of our canine companions. It's like having a script that covers the basics but might miss the nuanced elements that truly make a production shine.

In essence, the regulatory framework for pet food in the U.S. is a meticulous performance, ensuring safety and transparency, but as any pet parent knows, understanding and addressing the unique needs of our furry friends requires a bit more finesse. It's a symphony of federal and state efforts, yet the melody might need a bit of adjustment to truly harmonize with the dietary requirements of our beloved pets.

Unveiling the Regulatory Quirks in the Pet Food Arena

In the regulatory spectacle of pet food oversight in the United States, there are some intriguing plot twists that pet owners should be privy to:

- The FDA, while steering the pet food ship, allows for a bit of rule-bending through FDA policy. It's like having some flexible guidelines, allowing for a dance within the regulatory framework.

- AAFCO steps onto the stage with model language that states and governing bodies can adopt into law. However, it's crucial to note that AAFCO doesn't play the role of regulator, tester, approver, or certifier for pet food. It's more of a scriptwriter, providing a template for others to follow.

- Under the Food Drug and Cosmetic Act (FD&CA) of 1938, both human and animal food, including pet food, must be safe. However, the FD&C Act doesn't mandate that pet food meets specific nutritional adequacy standards. It's like ensuring the safety of the play without strictly dictating every nutritional nuance.

- Some pet food products aim to be more than just a meal; they're formulated as complete diets to address specific health issues. This adds a layer of complexity under the FD&C Act, allowing the FDA to regulate them as drugs, food, or a combination. Yet, the Compliance Policy Guide outlines the considerations the FDA weighs before cracking down on companies potentially selling these specialized pet foods illegally.

In essence, while pet food in the U.S. undergoes a regulatory *pas de deux*, it's essential for pet owners to grasp the fine print. Regulations might not always align perfectly with a pet's nutritional needs. Aware of these limitations, savvy pet parents might explore alternative options like homemade dog food or natural diets, ensuring their furry companions get the tailored nutrition they deserve.

Taking a Closer Look at the Regulatory Landscape of the U.S. Pet Food Industry

While regulatory bodies oversee pet food standards, it's crucial for pet owners and informed consumers to exercise a discerning eye. Regulatory measures are undoubtedly in place, yet blind acceptance can leave gaps in ensuring the well-being of our furry companions.

The complex interplay of policies and practices within these regulatory frameworks demands careful scrutiny. Pet owners, as the primary advocates for their pets' health, should delve deeper into understanding not just what regulations dictate but also their enforcement and potential limitations.

Scrutinizing ingredient lists, investigating sourcing practices, and staying informed about potential recalls or updates in regulations are integral parts of being an empowered pet parent. By questioning and seeking transparency, pet owners contribute to a culture of accountability in the pet food industry.

Remember, being an informed consumer isn't just a choice; it's a responsibility. It's a commitment to the well-being of our pets, ensuring that the food they consume aligns with the high standards of care and love we provide in every other aspect of their lives.

let's take a look at some of these agencies as they relate to the pet food industry.

FDA: The Primary Regulatory Player

The Food and Drug Administration (FDA) assumes the central role in governing the pet food industry within the United States.

Their key responsibilities encompass:

1. Rare Reviews: Occasional assessments of pet food manufacturing and ingredient suppliers, with the exclusion of those regulated by the USDA (for example, meat suppliers under USDA jurisdiction).

2. Pet Food Inspections: Conducting pet food inspections based on consumer or veterinary complaints.

3. Collaboration with AAFCO: Working in tandem with the Association of American Feed Control Officials (AAFCO) to develop state regulations. This includes defining ingredients and establishing nutritional requirements for pet food and animal feed.

4. Approval of Additives: Granting or denying approval for pet food additives or processing aids not specified by AAFCO, with a focus on Generally Recognized as Safe (GRAS) ingredients.

While the FDA is tasked with overseeing pet food regulations guided by federal laws such as the Food, Drug, and Cosmetic Act, the Food, Drug, and Cosmetic Amendments Act, and the Food Safety Modernization Act, challenges exist. Notably, the FDA's enforcement of regulations is not consistently stringent, and some aspects of pet food production might deviate from federal standards, a leniency allowed through FDA policy.

State Department of Agriculture: An Independent Authority

The State Department of Agriculture stands as an optional regulatory authority over pet food, sharing responsibilities with the FDA. Its duties include:

1. Registration Requirements: Many U.S. states mandate pet food producers to

annually register each product sold within state boundaries, often accompanied by fees.

2. Label Compliance: Some states inspect pet food labels for adherence to labeling regulations during the yearly registration process.

3. Random Testing: Certain states conduct random testing of pet food for harmful bacteria or to verify Guaranteed Analysis claims.

4. Complaint Investigations: Some states independently or in collaboration with the FDA investigate consumer complaints regarding pet food.

5. Manufacturing Facility Inspections: Inspection of pet food/treat manufacturing facilities by some states, either independently or in collaboration with the FDA.

6. AAFCO Collaboration: Collaboration with AAFCO to develop state regulations, define ingredients, and establish nutritional requirements for pet food/animal feed.

The State Department of Agriculture's regulation of pet food is guided by state regulation, operating in conjunction with federal regulation. However, enforcement varies, and some states may follow FDA cues when federal regulations are not strictly enforced.

AAFCO: A Regulatory Contributor

The Association of American Feed Control Officials (AAFCO) lacks direct regulatory power but plays a significant role. It is an independent association comprising members from State Departments of Agriculture and the FDA. AAFCO's contributions include:

1. Model Bills: Crafting Model Bills that are generally accepted as state regulations (though not universally adopted).

2. Nutritional Standards: Defining the nutritional requirements for cat and dog food to meet a Total and Balanced guarantee.

3. Ingredient Definitions: Outlining legal definitions for all pet food/animal feed ingredients.

4. Labeling Requirements: Establishing labeling requirements for pet food (information not publicly disclosed, owned by AAFCO).

USDA: Limited Oversight

The U.S. Department of Agriculture (USDA) lacks regulatory authority over pet food quality, production, marketing, or distribution. Responsibilities include:

1. Certification Program: Operating a voluntary pet food certification program not officially recognized by the FDA or State Department of Agriculture.

2. Meat Regulation: Regulating meat for human consumption under the Food Safety Inspection Services (FSIS) but not officially for pet use.

3. APHIS Oversight: Providing limited oversight of pet food exported outside the U.S. through the Animal Plant Health Inspection Services (APHIS).
In summary, while these regulatory bodies contribute to the oversight of the pet food industry, each has specific roles and limitations, creating a complex regulatory landscape. Enforcement may vary, and collaboration between federal and state entities is crucial for comprehensive regulation.

Doggie Health Challenges and Tailored Diets

Navigating the world of dog health can be as intricate as a delicate soufflé. Various common health issues demand a specialized culinary approach for our furry friends. Let's dissect a few examples:

1. Allergies and Intolerances:
Just like us, dogs can have dietary sensitivities. An exquisite diet might involve eliminating common allergens like beef, chicken, dairy, or grains.

2. Kidney Disease:
For our four-legged companions grappling with kidney issues, a refined menu might call for lower levels of protein, phosphorus, and sodium, alleviating the strain on those vital organs.

3. Battle of the Bulge - Obesity:
Addressing canine corpulence requires a masterfully crafted diet, lower in calories and fat, orchestrating a symphony to shed those excess pounds.

4. Pancreatitis Dance:
Dogs tangoing with pancreatitis benefit from a low-fat diet, a strategic move to minimize the risk of fiery flare-ups.

5. Dental Symphony:
For those with dental concertos, a softer or smaller-sized menu takes center stage, making it a breeze for them to chew and savor each note.

6. Skin and Coat Sonata:
Harmony for pups with skin and coat conditions lies in a diet rich in omega-3 fatty acids, a crescendo that enhances their skin and coat health.

7. Heartfelt Melody - Heart Disease:
Dogs with hearts that need a little extra love might find solace in a diet gently orchestrated with lower sodium, easing the strain on their tender hearts.

These examples merely scratch the surface of the myriad health intricacies our canine companions might face. If your furry friend finds themselves in a health conundrum requiring a specialized diet, collaborate with your trusted veterinarian. Together, you can compose a dietary opus that caters precisely to their nutritional needs, ensuring they savor each bite on the path to well-being.

Canine Culinary Quirks: Unmasking Allergens

In the gastronomic realm of our furry friends, allergies and intolerances often lurk like sneaky sous chefs. Let's unveil some common ingredients that can trigger a canine culinary conundrum:

1. Beef:
A surprising lead role in canine allergies, beef can orchestrate skin irritation, relentless itching, and digestive discord. Research, including a 2016 study by Mueller et al., crowned beef as the most reported food allergen in dogs, with a notable 34% displaying skin allergies when indulging in this meaty fare.

2. Dairy Drama:
Milk and cheese, while delectable to many, may unfold a tale of digestive discomfort, skin irritation, and incessant itching in our canine companions.

3. Wheat Woes:
A common antagonist in the canine culinary world, wheat takes center stage, bringing digestive disturbances, skin irritation, and an itch-inducing encore.

4. Chicken Chronicles:
Despite its popularity, chicken can be a troublesome character, inciting skin irritation, persistent itching, and digestive disquiet among our canine friends.

5. Egg Enigma:
Eggs, a breakfast staple for many, might unfold an enigma for dogs, triggering digestive unease, skin irritation, and the relentless urge to scratch.

6. Soy Saga:
Soy, a seemingly innocuous addition, plays the role of a common allergen, leading the canine culinary drama with digestive unrest, skin irritation, and an itching crescendo.

7. Corn
Corn is a common allergen in dogs, and can cause digestive upset, skin irritation, and itching.

8. Even, Beef
In the intricate tapestry of canine health, beef can unexpectedly emerge as a culinary nemesis for some dogs, triggering allergic reactions that echo throughout their well-being. These reactions often manifest as skin irritation, relentless itching, and digestive upset, revealing a complex interplay between canine palates and dietary discord. Research, notably a 2016 study by Mueller et al., underscores beef as a prevalent allergen, with 34% of food-allergic dogs showcasing skin allergies when exposed to this meaty culprit. Navigating this allergenic terrain necessitates a vigilant approach, prompting pet owners to explore alternative protein sources and scrutinize ingredient lists to craft a diet that orchestrates a harmonious symphony for their four-legged companions, free from the disruptive notes of beef-induced allergies.

Unraveling Canine Culinary Mysteries: Testing for Allergies

Concerns about allergies in dogs are not uncommon, prompting many pet owners to ponder the prevalence and the level of worry warranted. The reality is that allergies among our canine companions are not rare occurrences. Dogs can develop allergies or intolerances to various ingredients in their food, with common culprits including beef, dairy, wheat, chicken, eggs, and soy.

The degree of concern should be calibrated based on individual circumstances. If you observe persistent signs such as itching, digestive upset, or skin irritation in your dog, it's advisable to consult with your veterinarian. They can conduct tests, such as elimination diets, blood tests, or saliva tests, to identify potential allergens and tailor a suitable diet plan. While allergies are part of the diverse spectrum of canine health, proactive veterinary guidance can navigate these challenges and help ensure your furry friend thrives on a diet tailored to their unique nutritional needs.'

When it comes to deciphering the intricate web of food allergies or intolerances in our canine companions, several testing methods come into play:

1. Elimination Diet:
Considered the gold standard, an elimination diet involves a meticulous food trial spanning eight to twelve weeks. This process entails feeding your dog a hypoallergenic diet featuring a novel protein and carbohydrate source they haven't encountered before. Gradual reintroduction of other foods helps pinpoint the allergen responsible for the adverse reactions.

2. Blood Tests:
Blood tests offer insights into specific food allergies by measuring antibodies present in the blood. While they can identify potential allergens, these tests may not always be foolproof and are recommended alongside other diagnostic methods.

3. Saliva Tests:
Similar to blood tests, saliva tests gauge antibodies to specific foods in dogs. While they provide additional data, their reliability varies, making them most effective when combined with other diagnostic approaches.

4. At-Home Allergy Tests:
Convenience meets curiosity with at-home allergy tests, which involve collecting saliva or fur samples for laboratory analysis. While these tests offer a DIY approach, their accuracy may fluctuate, necessitating a complementary use of other diagnostic methods.

It's crucial to emphasize that suspicion of food allergies or intolerances in your dog should prompt collaboration with your veterinarian. Together, you can unravel the culinary conundrum, pinpoint the cause, and sculpt a tailored diet plan that aligns with your furry friend's unique nutritional needs.

The Culinary Remedy: Decoding Hypoallergenic Diets for Dogs

A hypoallergenic diet for dogs is a culinary game-changer, featuring a novel protein source rarely found in conventional dog foods, think venison or duck. Simple and straightforward, this dog food embraces uncomplicated ingredients like fruits and vegetables, boasting a refreshingly concise list compared to its counterparts. Let's break down the key elements:

1. Novel Protein Source:
 - Embracing unconventional proteins like venison or duck sets this diet apart, steering clear of common allergens.

2. Simple Ingredients:
 - Fruits and vegetables take center stage, contributing to a straightforward and nourishing canine cuisine.

3. Allergen-Free Zone:
 - Bid farewell to beef, chicken, dairy, wheat, and soy – common allergens that are notably absent.

4. Limited Ingredient Diet (LID):
 - Simplifying the tracking of your dog's dietary intake, LID ensures a focused and manageable approach.

5. Grain-Free Advantage:
 - With an eye on digestive well-being, the absence of grains minimizes the risk of upset stomachs.

Tailored for dogs grappling with food allergies or intolerances, hypoallergenic dog food emerges as a strategic ally. If suspicions arise regarding your dog's dietary challenges, collaborate with your veterinarian to pinpoint the cause and devise a nutritional plan tailored to their unique needs. A hypoallergenic diet may just be the palatable prescription your furry companion requires.

The Hypoallergenic Dilemma: Weighing the Pros and Cons

Introducing a hypoallergenic diet to your furry companion can indeed be a boon for those grappling with food allergies or intolerances. However, navigating this culinary landscape requires careful consideration of potential risks. Here's the lowdown:

1. Nutritional Deficiencies:
 - The allure of hypoallergenic diets lies in their potential to alleviate food allergies or intolerances in dogs. However, amid the pursuit of allergy relief, there's a potential pitfall—nutritional deficiencies. Hypoallergenic diets, with their narrowed ingredient profiles, may inadvertently lack some vital nutrients essential for your dog's overall health. It's a nuanced balance between addressing specific sensitivities and ensuring a comprehensive nutrient intake.

To mitigate the risk of nutritional gaps, opting for a top-tier hypoallergenic diet becomes crucial. High-quality formulations are crafted with precision, aiming to provide a well-rounded nutritional profile that aligns with your dog's needs. Collaborating closely with your veterinarian adds an extra layer of assurance. Together, you can tailor a nutritionally complete plan, bridging potential deficiencies and safeguarding against unintended health implications. Remember, the success of a hypoallergenic diet hinges not just on its allergy-alleviating properties but on its ability to deliver comprehensive nutrition for your dog's overall well-being.

2. Cost Considerations:
- The price tag of hypoallergenic diets can be higher than their conventional counterparts, posing a financial hurdle for some pet owners.

3. Limited Ingredient Diets (LIDs):
- Limited Ingredient Diets (LIDs) have become synonymous with hypoallergenic dog food, offering a focused approach to dietary management. These specialized diets intentionally keep the ingredient list concise, aiming to address food allergies and intolerances. However, the very essence of a limited ingredient approach can pose a nutritional challenge. The deliberate restriction of components, while beneficial in managing specific health issues, may inadvertently limit the spectrum of essential nutrients your dog receives. This underscores the critical need for strategic planning in crafting a well-rounded diet that compensates for potential nutrient gaps. Collaborating with your veterinarian becomes paramount, ensuring that the LID chosen meets your dog's unique nutritional requirements. While LIDs can be a powerful tool in managing dietary sensitivities, thoughtful consideration and expert guidance are vital to strike the right balance for your furry friend's overall health.

4. Pathogen Contamination Risks:
- Raw or freeze-dried hypoallergenic diets share the same pathogen contamination risks as other raw options. Prudent handling and storage are paramount to mitigate bacterial threats.

5. Food Intolerances:
- While adept at curbing food allergies, hypoallergenic diets may not prove effective for dogs with food intolerances. Collaborate with your vet to pinpoint the cause and tailor a diet plan accordingly.

In essence, while hypoallergenic diets offer a lifeline for dogs with specific dietary challenges, the key lies in selecting a premium, well-balanced option and working closely with your veterinarian to secure your dog's overall well-being.'

Essential Take-Aways When Considering the Hypo-Allergenic Route

In the realm of hypoallergenic dog food, navigating the options demands the precision of a surgeon. Here's a no-nonsense guide to make sure you're not playing Russian roulette with your pet's nutrition:

1. Consult with your veterinarian:
   Your first port of call – the vet. Seek their counsel to ascertain if a hypoallergenic diet aligns with your dog's needs. They're the experts, after all.

2. Look for a limited ingredient diet (LID):
   Keep it simple. LID dog food trims the ingredient list, aiding in tracking your dog's intake and minimizing the risk of allergic fallout.

3. Choose a novel protein source:
   Novelty is key. Opt for proteins like venison, duck, or kangaroo – something your dog's taste buds haven't swirled around before.

4. Avoid common allergens:
   Kick out the troublemakers. Ensure your chosen hypoallergenic dog food is a safe zone, devoid of beef, chicken, dairy, wheat, and soy.

5. Read the ingredient label:
   Sherlock Holmes mode: ON. Scrutinize that label. Make sure it's not just hypoallergenic but a comprehensive, nutrient-packed package for your furry friend.

6. Consider your budget:
   Money talks, even in the dog food aisle. Mind your purse strings – hypoallergenic might cost a bit more, so weigh your options wisely.

7. Try different brands and formulations:
   Be open to exploration. It might take a bit of trial and error, so don't be afraid to shuffle through brands until you find the one that hits the sweet spot.

In the symphony of hypoallergenic dog food, orchestrate your choices with the precision of a maestro, considering your dog's unique needs and dietary nuances. The vet's guidance and a discerning eye on the ingredient label are your tools to ensure your pet feasts on the right notes. No compromise. No shortcuts. Just a commitment to your dog's well-being.

Vital Veterinarian Guidance: The Unavoidable Necessity When Navigating Hypoallergenic Diets for Your Dog

Considering a leap into the realm of hypoallergenic diets for your dog? Think twice before navigating this culinary journey alone. Here's the unspoken truth – it's not advisable to embark on the hypoallergenic adventure sans a veterinarian's guidance. Let's dissect the reasons:

1. Accurate Diagnosis:
One of the pivotal aspects of implementing a hypoallergenic diet for your dog is the need for an accurate diagnosis, and there's no one better equipped to provide this than a veterinarian. Dogs, like humans, can exhibit various symptoms that may suggest food allergies or intolerances, such as skin irritations, itching, or digestive issues. A veterinarian possesses the expertise to discern whether these symptoms are indeed indicative of a food-related concern or if there may be other underlying health issues at play. Attempting to switch to a hypoallergenic diet without this precise diagnosis can be akin to navigating in the dark – it might not address the root cause, potentially leading to unaddressed health problems for your furry companion. Therefore, seeking the guidance of a veterinarian ensures a thorough and accurate assessment, laying the foundation for an effective and tailored dietary plan for your dog's specific needs.

2. Nutritional Balance:
Your vet transforms into a nutritional wizard, ensuring the alchemical mix of your dog's hypoallergenic diet is spot-on. Without this expertise, the nutritional scales could tip into imbalance, jeopardizing your dog's well-being.

3. Gradual Transition:
Like a maestro orchestrating a symphony, your vet guides the gradual transition to the new diet. Hastening this process could lead to a cacophony of gastrointestinal issues – vomiting, diarrhea, and diminished appetite.

4. Cost Considerations:
Your vet, acting as a financial advisor, navigates the fiscal waters of hypoallergenic diets. While these diets might strain your wallet, your vet helps you pick an option that aligns with both your dog's needs and your budget.

In essence, before delving into the world of hypoallergenic diets, consult your vet – the seasoned captain who ensures a safe and healthy passage for your furry companion. It's not just about diet; it's about a tailored culinary journey crafted for your dog's well-being.

Choosing a Raw Diet for Your Pooch: A Critical Analysis

Raw food diets have gained popularity in the canine culinary scene, but before you embark on this trend, let's dissect the matter. Here's the lowdown:

Pros of a raw food diet for dogs:

- A raw food diet aligns with a dog's natural and biologically appropriate eating habits.

- Tailorability allows you to meet your dog's specific nutritional needs.

- Some dogs with food sensitivities may find solace in a raw food diet.

- A shinier coat, healthier skin, and an overall health boost can be attributed to a raw food diet.

Cons of a raw food diet for dogs:

- The preparation of raw food diets can be a financial and time-consuming commitment.

- Handling raw meat poses a bacterial contamination risk, posing dangers to both dogs and their human counterparts.

- The nutritional balance of raw food diets may be lacking, potentially leading to health issues.

- Digestive upset may be a concern for some dogs grappling with raw food.

Now, let's take a closer look at the alternative culinary path: cooking for your canine companion. The prospect of preparing meals for your furry friend comes with its own set of considerations and advantages. Cooking allows you to have precise control over the ingredients, ensuring a well-rounded and balanced diet tailored to your dog's specific nutritional needs. It also provides the opportunity to address any dietary restrictions or health concerns your dog might have.

Additionally, the cooking process can enhance the digestibility of certain ingredients, making nutrients more accessible to your dog's system. It's a chance to incorporate a variety of proteins, vegetables, and grains, offering a diverse and palatable menu. While the time and effort invested in cooking may be greater than opting for commercial dog food, the rewards in terms of your dog's health and happiness can be substantial.

Importantly, consulting with your veterinarian during this culinary exploration is key. They can provide valuable insights into crafting a balanced and nutritious homemade diet, ensuring your dog thrives on the carefully curated meals. So, before venturing into the "raw" realm, consider the option of whipping up wholesome and delicious cooked meals for your beloved canine companion.

3 Cooking for Your Dog: Food Basics

Food Safety

Alright, let's dive into the basics of food safety when preparing meals for your canine pal. Just like in any professional kitchen, cleanliness and hygiene are non-negotiable. First off, wash your hands thoroughly before and after handling any ingredients. Now, onto the ingredients – they need to be fresh, high-quality, and suitable for canine consumption. Check for any recalls or advisories on pet food ingredients.

When it comes to meat, keep it separate from other ingredients and ensure it's cooked thoroughly to eliminate any potential pathogens. Cross-contamination is a culinary tightrope that demands utmost attention, a non-negotiable aspect when orchestrating meals for your cherished canine companion. In the realm of food preparation, cross-contamination occurs when harmful microorganisms, be it bacteria or pathogens, unwittingly hitch a ride from one surface or substance to another. Let's paint a vivid scenario: you're diligently dicing raw meat to concoct a sumptuous dinner for your pup. Now, in a culinary misstep, you decide to repurpose the same cutting board for slicing up fresh vegetables without a thorough cleanse. A dangerous game of microbial musical chairs begins.

To mitigate this risk, a golden rule emerges: segregation is key. Designate specific cutting boards and utensils for the exclusive use of your dog's culinary creations. If raw meat graces your counter-top, let it not mingle with other ingredients without a meticulous interlude of cleaning. Imagine it as running a top-tier kitchen, where meticulous organization, unwavering cleanliness, and an acute awareness of potential hazards reign supreme. By standing guard against cross-contamination, you're not merely crafting delectable dishes; you're safeguarding your dog's meals from any potential culinary hitchhikers, ensuring a gastronomic experience that is both delightful and risk-free.

Storage is critical – refrigerate or freeze portions promptly, and avoid leaving food out for extended periods. Remember, the same rules you follow for your food apply to your pup's. It's all about respect for the ingredients and a commitment to their well-being. Keep it clean, keep it safe, and create meals that'll have your dog's tail wagging with delight.

§

Mastering the Art of Freezing and Thawing: Ensuring Canine Culinary Perfection

Ensuring the safety and quality of homemade dog food is a culinary responsibility that extends to freezing and reheating practices. Picture this: a well-prepared batch of nourishing canine cuisine, meticulously crafted to meet your dog's specific nutritional needs. Yet, the artistry doesn't end with the creation; it extends to preservation.

When freezing homemade dog food, embark on this culinary journey armed with airtight containers or vacuum-sealed bags, the unsung heroes that thwart freezer burn and contamination. Labeling and dating these vessels serve as the navigational stars, guiding you through the vastness of your freezer with precision. Opt for small portions, a strategic move to thaw only what your furry friend needs, reducing waste and preserving freshness.

Now, the inevitable question arises—how long does this frozen masterpiece endure? Most homemade dog food recipes gracefully stand the test of time for three to six months in the freezer, provided they bask in the protective embrace of proper storage.

The thawing process, a symphony of caution, demands strategic choreography. In the refrigerator, the safest stage for this performance, takes a measured 12 to 36 hours, the slow dance of preservation. Alternatively, the cold water ballet involves placing the frozen treasure in a waterproof bag, submerged in a bowl of cold water, refreshed every 30 minutes. For those in a hurry, the cold-water bath technique, where the pan, water, and frozen delight collide, shaves off time but requires vigilance.

Let's be crystal clear on one culinary decree: never defrost homemade dog food at room temperature or in hot water. These arenas birth bacteria, harbingers of foodborne illnesses. Instead, embrace the slow thaw, the cold water ballet, or the brisk cold-water bath for a culinary encore that's both safe and delectable. As you embark on this gastronomic journey, remember, your vet is the trusted navigator, ensuring your canine companion's diet is not just a meal but a masterpiece.

§

Masterful Handling of Homemade Dog Fare: Freezing and Reheating Techniques

Crafting your dog's meals with care and foresight involves not only culinary prowess but also meticulous attention to food safety. Yes, you can prepare wholesome dog food in advance and freeze it for convenience, but excellence in this process requires precision. Let's delve into the art of preserving homemade dog food:

1. Hermetic Guardians: Airtight Containers Rule the Realm

When storing your culinary creations for your canine companion, embrace the use of airtight containers or reliable resealable bags. These culinary guardians shield the doggy delicacies from freezer burn, ensuring that each bite retains its delectable quality. A well-sealed fortress is the key to preserving the freshness and flavor that your dog deserves.

2. Time-Stamped Vigilance: Label and Date for Wisdom

In the realm of frozen culinary treasures, maintaining order is paramount. Label each container or bag with the meal's content and the date of its entrance into the icy sanctuary. This diligent record-keeping serves as your guide, allowing you to monitor the duration of each meal's frozen slumber. Remember, precision is the path to culinary triumph.

3. Petite Portion Paradigm: Freeze in Small Batches for Optimal Enjoyment

To ensure the pinnacle of freshness, adopt the strategy of freezing homemade dog food in small, manageable portions. This culinary wisdom minimizes waste, as you can thaw precisely what your dog needs for each meal. Embracing this portion-centric approach not only prevents unnecessary discard but also maintains the integrity of the food, leaving your dog's taste buds dancing with delight.

4. Vacuum Sealing Mastery: Fortifying Against Freezer Adversities

For the ultimate defense against the arch-nemesis of frozen foods – freezer burn – enlist the assistance of vacuum-sealed bags. These culinary marvels create an impermeable barrier, preserving the texture, flavor, and nutritional goodness of your homemade dog cuisine. In the realm of frozen doggy delights, a vacuum-sealed stronghold ensures that every thawed bite is a culinary triumph.

5. Frozen Elegance: Storing for Extended Culinary Gratification

While the icy confines of your freezer are a bastion of preservation, even they have limits. Most homemade dog food recipes can endure this frozen hibernation for a commendable three to six months. However, the key lies in judicious storage and adherence to the aforementioned principles. A symbiotic partnership with your veterinarian ensures that the frozen feast maintains its nutritional balance, catering to your dog's unique dietary needs.

In the culinary saga of freezing and reheating, precision, and culinary mastery reign supreme. Consult with your trusted veterinarian to orchestrate a harmonious dietary symphony that elevates your dog's dining experience to new heights.

§

Cautionary Measures: Reheating Frozen Dog Food in a Microwave

Defrosting homemade dog food in the microwave might seem like a quick fix, but it comes with potential drawbacks. Here's why you should think twice:

1. Bacterial Growth: Unwelcome Risks in Microwave Defrosting

One major concern when using the microwave to thaw homemade dog food is the heightened risk of bacterial growth. Unlike controlled thawing methods, microwaving may not uniformly raise the temperature of the food, creating pockets where bacteria can thrive. This uneven heating increases the chances of foodborne illnesses, potentially harming both your dog and anyone handling the food. To prioritize your pet's health, opt for safer thawing alternatives.

2. Nutrient Loss: Microwaving and the Erosion of Nutritional Value

The microwave's intense heat can contribute to the loss of essential nutrients in homemade dog food. The process of defrosting and reheating may degrade vitamins, minerals, and other crucial elements, diminishing the overall nutritional value of the meal. Since a well-balanced diet is key to your dog's health, it's imperative to choose thawing methods that preserve the food's nutritional integrity. Your veterinarian can guide you on safe alternatives that ensure your dog receives optimal nutrition.

3. Uneven Heating: A Recipe for Mouth Burns in Your Dog

Microwaving homemade dog food poses the risk of uneven heating, leading to the formation of hot spots within the food. These unevenly heated areas can be dangerously hot, potentially causing burns to your dog's mouth and tongue. Such injuries can be painful and lead to aversions to certain foods or difficulties in eating. To safeguard your pet, consider alternative thawing methods like the refrigerator or cold-water bath, which provide more controlled and uniform warming. Prioritizing your dog's safety during meal preparation is an essential aspect of responsible pet care.

For a safer approach, opt for defrosting in the refrigerator or through a cold-water bath. In the refrigerator, transfer the frozen dog food directly and allow 12 to 36 hours for thawing, depending on the quantity and refrigerator temperature. Alternatively, use a cold-water bath by submerging the sealed bag of frozen food in a bowl of cold water, refreshing the water every 30 minutes. Regular checks ensure complete thawing, typically taking 20 to 30 minutes for a portion.

Crucially, avoid defrosting at room temperature or in hot water, as these methods heighten the risk of bacterial growth and foodborne illness. Always adhere to safe food handling practices and consult your veterinarian if you harbor any concerns about your dog's diet.

§

Urgent Refreezing Protocols: A Culinary Imperative

Listen up, because when it comes to refreezing homemade dog food, precision is not just a suggestion—it's an absolute culinary imperative. Here are the hard-hitting guidelines you need to follow to ensure the safety and quality of your dog's culinary delights:

1. Race Against Time: Refreeze within the 2-3 Day Window

Time is of the essence, and you're on the clock. Refreeze that homemade dog food within a tight 2-3 day window after its chilly sojourn in the refrigerator. This swift action maintains the freshness and quality your dog deserves. No room for dilly-dallying in the world of frozen feasts.

2. Container Commandments: Airtight Armor Against the Elements

In the frosty arena of frozen preservation, the choice of containers or bags is nothing short of a strategic maneuver, and abiding by the Container Commandments ensures your culinary creations emerge unscathed from the battle against freezer burn and contamination. Let's delve into the expanded wisdom of these airtight guidelines:

A. Airtight Alchemy: The Sealing Ritual

When you choose airtight containers or the most resilient resealable bags, you're essentially performing a sealing ritual that transforms your kitchen creations into frost-resistant treasures. The alchemy of airtightness ensures that no frigid intruders, in the form of icy crystals or contaminants, can breach the fortress and compromise the integrity of your dog's delectable delights.

B. Culinary Armor: Guarding Against Freezer Burn

Freezer burn, the arch-nemesis of frozen feasts, seeks to desiccate and distort. Your airtight containers or fortified bags act as the impenetrable armor, standing guard against the malevolent forces of dehydration and oxidation. They shield your culinary treasures, ensuring that every bite your dog takes is as succulent and flavorful as the day it was crafted.

C. Contamination Conundrum: Foiling the Frosty Foes

Contamination, a stealthy infiltrator, lurks in the icy shadows. Airtight containers and robust resealable bags form an unassailable defense, preventing any foreign entities from compromising the purity of your homemade dog food. It's a culinary seal of approval, declaring that only the finest ingredients shall grace your dog's dish.

D. Seal the Flavor, Seal the Quality: A Covenant of Excellence

The sealing act goes beyond mere protection; it's a covenant of excellence. As you seal the flavor within and guard the quality with airtight precision, you're setting a standard of culinary distinction. It's a promise that each thawed portion will be a testament to your dedication to canine gastronomy.

E. The Sacred Deal: A Pact With Culinary Integrity

When you seal the deal with airtight containers, you're entering a sacred pact with culinary integrity. It's a commitment to uphold the quality, freshness, and nutritional value of your homemade dog food. Your choice of containers becomes a symbol of your unwavering dedication to the well-being and delight of your four-legged friend.

In the grand symphony of frozen storage, the Container Commandments resonate as a guiding melody. As you armor your culinary creations with airtight precision, you're not just preserving food; you're orchestrating a culinary masterpiece that awaits the eager palate of your loyal canine companion."

3. Chronicles of the Frozen Kingdom: Label and Date with Authority

Every container or bag in your frozen arsenal needs a badge of honor. Label and date each one with military precision. This isn't just record-keeping; it's a manifesto for maintaining the integrity of your dog's meals. Know the age, respect the vintage.

4. One Shot, No Replay: Refreeze Only Once, No Exceptions

Let this be your culinary mantra: one thaw, one refreeze. Don't play games with the nutritional value and quality of your dog's sustenance. Multiple rounds of thawing and refreezing are a culinary gamble you can't afford.

5. Thawing Symphony: Refrigerator or Cold-Water Overture, No Room for Error

The thawing process is a delicate ballet—choose your stage wisely. Whether in the refrigerator's cold embrace or the brisk cold-water bath, avoid the pitfalls of room temperature or microwave thawing. Precision in thawing ensures the symphony of flavors your dog deserves.

In the grand tapestry of frozen cuisine, these guidelines are your culinary commandments. They're not suggestions; they're absolutes. The nutritional balance and well-being of your dog rest on your culinary prowess. Consult with your trusted veterinarian to ensure that every refreeze aligns with your dog's unique dietary needs. This is not just cooking; this is a culinary responsibility of the highest order.

§

Preservation Protocol: Labeling Your Canine Cuisine for the Freezer Fray

When it comes to freezing homemade dog food, the battle is not just about sealing freshness—it's also a war on forgetfulness. Proper labeling is your arsenal, and here's your battle plan to ensure victory in the freezer fray:

1. Tactical Precision: Deploy the Permanent Marker
Don't bring a pen to a marker fight. Arm yourself with a permanent marker, a Sharpie perhaps, to etch your labels onto containers or bags. This isn't just about identification; it's about leaving an indelible mark in the cold archives of your freezer. No smudging, no compromise.

2. Date and Identity: Name of the Game
Your labels should tell a story—name of the food and the date it was made. This is no time for ambiguity. Scribble down the culinary genealogy on each container or bag. Knowing your dog's meal lineage ensures you use the oldest treasures first. Name and date—non-negotiable.

3. Allergen Alert: Include the Ingredients
In the world of canine cuisine, knowledge is power. If your dog has dietary sensitivities or allergies, the label must spill the beans on ingredients. This information isn't just for you; it's a protective shield against potential culinary skirmishes. List those ingredients with pride and precision.

4. Cold-Proof Labels: Freezer-Grade or Bust
Labels that shiver and crumble in the cold have no place in the freezer domain. Arm yourself with freezer-grade labels, resilient soldiers that stand firm against the icy winds of frost. No compromise on durability; these labels are your culinary sentinels.

5. Frozen Citadel: Strategic Storage in the Coolest Recesses

In the grand theater of frozen warfare, the battle for optimal storage is akin to choosing the ideal fortress for your culinary creations. Here's an expanded directive on why selecting the coldest recesses of your freezer is the pinnacle of strategic storage:

A. The Hierarchy of Coldness: Understanding Your Freezer's Landscape
Freezers are not homogeneous icy landscapes; they have hierarchies of coldness. The upper shelves near the door experience temperature fluctuations every time it swings open, making them the warmest territories. The real deep freeze, the coldest recesses, lies in the lower regions and towards the back.

B. Chilling Preservation: Maintaining Temperature Uniformity

Storing your labeled containers or bags in the coolest recesses ensures that the temperature remains consistently low. Temperature uniformity is crucial to prevent thawing and refreezing cycles that can compromise the texture and quality of your meticulously prepared canine cuisine.

C. Shielding from Thawing Threats: A Barrier Against Temperature Fluctuations

The door of your freezer might be a high-traffic zone, with frequent openings and closings. Placing your labeled treasures in the coolest recesses acts as a protective barrier against the thawing threats induced by temperature fluctuations. It's your way of shielding your frozen assets from the warmth seeking in.

D. Extended Freshness: Prolonging the Lifespan of Your Culinary Creations

Like a well-fortified citadel, the coldest recesses serve as a stronghold against the relentless march of time. It's a place where your canine delicacies can maintain their frozen freshness for an extended period. Your frozen citadel becomes a time capsule, preserving flavors and nutrients until the next culinary campaign.

E. Efficient Retrieval: Ready for Culinary Quests

Storing your labeled containers strategically means they are in prime position for efficient retrieval. No more digging through frosty archives; your frozen citadel allows you to swiftly locate and retrieve the culinary provisions for your loyal companion's next feast.

In the realm of frozen storage, the coolest recesses are the unsung heroes, silently safeguarding the integrity of your homemade dog food. It's a tactical decision that goes beyond mere placement; it's a commitment to culinary excellence and canine well-being. As you embark on this frozen culinary journey, let your labeled treasures find refuge in the coldest citadel of your freezer—a testament to your commitment to quality and care.

Remember, labeling is not just about order; it's a strategic maneuver to safeguard the nutritional balance and well-being of your canine companion. Consult with your trusted veterinarian to ensure your labeling strategy aligns with your dog's unique dietary needs. This is not just preservation; it's a culinary pact with your loyal friend.

4 How Much to Feed?

When determining how much food to feed your dog based on their optimal weight, it is important to consider several factors, including their age, activity level, and metabolic rate.

Here are some general guidelines for how much to feed your dog based on their weight:

1. Small Breeds (3-20 pounds): 1/3 to 1 1/2 cups per day, depending on their weight and age.

2. Medium Breeds (21-50 pounds): 1 3/4 to 2 2/3 cups per day, depending on their weight and age.

3. Large Breeds (60-100 pounds): 3 to 4 1/2 cups per day, plus 1/3 cup for every 10 pounds over 100 pounds.

4. X-Large Breeds (over 100 pounds): 5 1/4 cups plus 1/3 cup for every 10 pounds over 100 pounds.

It is important to note that these are general guidelines and that individual dogs may require more or less food depending on their individual needs. It is also important to consult with a veterinarian to determine the optimal feeding amount for your dog based on their age, weight, and activity level. Additionally, it is important to divide the recommended daily amount of food into multiple meals throughout the day to prevent overeating and promote healthy digestion.

Finally, it is important to factor in the caloric content of any treats, table scraps, or supplements you give your dog to ensure that they are not consuming too many calories and gaining weight.

Here is a list of the top 50 dog breeds with optimal weight associated with each:

1. Labrador Retriever: 55-80 pounds
2. German Shepherd: 50-90 pounds
3. Golden Retriever: 55-75 pounds
4. French Bulldog: 16-28 pounds
5. Bulldog: 40-50 pounds
6. Beagle: 18-30 pounds
7. Poodle (Standard): 45-70 pounds
8. Rottweiler: 80-135 pounds
9. Siberian Husky: 35-60 pounds
10. Boxer: 50-70 pounds
11. Dachshund: 11-32 pounds
12. Shih Tzu: 9-16 pounds
13. Doberman Pinscher: 60-100 pounds
14. Australian Shepherd: 40-65 pounds
15. Great Dane: 110-175 pounds
16. Miniature Schnauzer: 11-20 pounds
17. Chihuahua: 2-6 pounds
18. Shetland Sheepdog: 15-25 pounds
19. Border Collie: 30-55 pounds
20. Cocker Spaniel: 20-30 pounds
21. Boxer: 50-70 pounds
22. Akita: 70-130 pounds
23. Yorkshire Terrier: 4-7 pounds
24. Cavalier King Charles Spaniel: 13-18 pounds
25. Pomeranian: 3-7 pounds
26. Basset Hound: 40-65 pounds
27. Bullmastiff: 100-130 pounds
28. Pug: 14-18 pounds
29. Bernese Mountain Dog: 70-115 pounds
30. Alaskan Malamute: 85-100 pounds
31. Dalmatian: 45-70 pounds
32. Staffordshire Bull Terrier: 24-38 pounds
33. Weimaraner: 55-90 pounds
34. Collie: 50-70 pounds
35. West Highland White Terrier: 15-20 pounds
36. Newfoundland: 100-150 pounds
37. Havanese: 7-13 pounds
38. Shiba Inu: 17-23 pounds
39. Whippet: 25-40 pounds
40. Scottish Terrier: 18-22 pounds
41. Papillon: 5-10 pounds
42. Boston Terrier: 12-25 pounds
43. Akita: 70-130 pounds
44. Vizsla: 45-65 pounds
45. Rhodesian Ridgeback: 70-85 pounds
46. Chesapeake Bay Retriever: 55-80 pounds
47. Italian Greyhound: 6-15 pounds
48. Bull Terrier: 35-75 pounds
49. Samoyed: 50-80 pounds
50. Portuguese Water Dog: 35-60 pounds

Remember, these are general guidelines, and individual dogs may fall outside these ranges. Consult with your vet for personalized advice based on your dog's health, age, and lifestyle.

A Sample One-Week Menu For Dogs Eating Homemade Food

In the section following our discussion of Bone Broth, we provide a complete 52-week recipe guide, but this is a good list to review when thinking about cooking for your dog, at home.

Day 1:
- Breakfast: Ground organic turkey thigh with finely chopped carrots and green beans
- Lunch: Brown rice with shredded chicken and steamed broccoli
- Dinner: Ground beef with sweet potato and spinach

Day 2:
- Breakfast: Scrambled eggs with cooked quinoa and blueberries
- Lunch: Turkey meatballs with zucchini and brown rice
- Dinner: Salmon with sweet potato and green beans

Day 3:
- Breakfast: Ground chicken with cooked oatmeal and strawberries
- Lunch: Beef stew with carrots and green beans
- Dinner: Ground turkey with cooked lentils and kale

Day 4:
- Breakfast: Cottage cheese with cooked pumpkin and apples
- Lunch: Chicken and rice with steamed carrots and peas
- Dinner: Ground beef with cooked barley and asparagus

Day 5:
- Breakfast: Greek yogurt with cooked sweet potato and blueberries
- Lunch: Turkey chili with cooked quinoa and green beans
- Dinner: Ground chicken with cooked brown rice and spinach

Day 6:
- Breakfast: Scrambled eggs with cooked sweet potato and raspberries
- Lunch: Beef and barley soup with carrots and green beans
- Dinner: Ground turkey with cooked lentils and kale

Day 7:
- Breakfast: Cottage cheese with cooked pumpkin and strawberries
- Lunch: Chicken and rice with steamed carrots and peas
- Dinner: Ground beef with cooked barley and asparagus

It is important to note that homemade dog food should be nutritionally balanced and meet your dog's specific nutritional needs. Consult with your veterinarian to determine the appropriate diet for your dog and to ensure that your homemade dog food is complete and balanced.

5 BONE BROTH: THE OVERVIEW

Bone Broth: The Culinary Cornerstone in Our Canine Feast

When it comes to crafting a culinary castle fit for your canine royalty, let's establish the cornerstone: bone broth. Think of it as the rich elixir that forms the foundation of the gastronomic masterpiece we're building throughout this book. Bone broth, a venerable stock born from the alchemy of simmering animal bones and connective tissues, is a nutrient-dense powerhouse that has stood the test of time.

Diving into the broth kingdom, we encounter various realms, each with its own unique flavor and nutritional profile. Poultry, game, beef, and fish—all offer a distinct journey for the palate. For our royal hounds, let's focus on the dynamic duo: chicken and beef bone broth.

Chicken Bone Broth: The Versatile Virtuoso

Picture chicken bone broth as the versatile virtuoso of the canine culinary symphony. Rich in type II collagen, a potent remedy for osteoarthritis and joint pain, it stands tall in the protein arena, offering a milder flavor that effortlessly integrates into any dish. Chicken bone broth isn't just about taste; it brings ascetic benefits to the royal table, enhancing the overall gastronomic experience.

Beef Bone Broth: The Gut Guardian

Now, turn your attention to beef bone broth, the gallant gut guardian in our culinary tale. Mostly composed of type III collagen, a glycine-packed ally that lays the groundwork for resilient connective tissues in the gut, beef bone broth is the superior choice for gut health. Laden with essential minerals—calcium, magnesium, phosphorus, and sulfur—it's a powerhouse that elevates energy levels and fortifies against inflammation. The bolder, more distinct flavor of beef bone broth makes a statement, leaving an indelible mark on your canine's royal feast.

The Royal Choice: A Matter of Preference and Well-being

In this culinary quest, the choice between chicken and beef bone broth becomes a matter of royal preference and specific nutritional needs. Chicken bone broth, with its protein prowess and ascetic allure, caters to those seeking a well-rounded canine banquet. On the other hand, beef bone broth, with its emphasis on gut health and mood elevation, beckons to the discerning connoisseur.

A Healthful Conclusion: The Majestic Merits of Both

In the grand finale, the verdict is clear: whether you opt for the versatile chicken or the robust beef bone broth, both promise a regal array of health and wellness benefits fit for the most discerning canine palate. Whichever path you tread in this culinary kingdom, rest assured that the royal banquet for your four-legged sovereign is poised for greatness, with bone broth as the crowning glory.

Bone Broth Unveiled: Elevate Your Dog's Dining Experience

Embarking on the journey of incorporating bone broth into your dog's culinary repertoire is more than a mere addition—it's a culinary elevation. Let's explore the rich tapestry of benefits that this liquid gold brings to your canine companion's bowl:

1. Nutrient-Rich Royalty:

- Bone broth reigns supreme in nutrition, boasting a royal blend of vitamins and minerals that bolster your dog's immune system and overall well-being.
- Packed with protein, collagen, glycine, and glucosamine, it delivers a nutritional punch that transcends the ordinary.

2. Gut Wellness Guard:

- A staunch defender of gut health, bone broth takes a stand against the notorious "leaky gut" condition.
- The gelatin within its depths supports robust digestion, proving a boon for dogs grappling with irritable and inflammatory bowel conditions.

3. Joint Health Monarch:

- The coronation of bone broth as the monarch of joint health is justified. Laden with glucosamine, chondroitin, and hyaluronic acid, it promotes the growth of collagen—an essential player in joint health.
- Bow before its prowess in alleviating joint pain and inflammation, bestowing a regal touch to your dog's mobility.

4. Hydration Sovereign:

- A hydration sovereign in the realm of dog diets, bone broth beckons to those discerning canines who turn a disdainful eye towards water.
- Perfect for replenishing nutrients during bouts of gastrointestinal unrest, bone broth stands tall as the elixir of hydration.

5. Skin and Coat Elegance:

- Bone broth weaves a tapestry of elegance, offering a rich source of collagen—a cornerstone in the realm of skin and coat health.
- Infused with skin-loving minerals like zinc and copper, it becomes the secret potion for a lustrous, regal coat.

Choosing Wisely:

When introducing bone broth to your dog's culinary kingdom, exercise discernment. Opt for varieties laden with natural, dog-safe ingredients, and steer clear of impostors laden with additives like onions, garlic, or salt. Remember, it's not about ubiquity; it's about a curated addition to a complete and balanced diet for your canine companion.

A Culinary Disclaimer:

- The grandeur of bone broth need not dominate every dish. The recipes in the menu section of this regal book treat bone broth as a last-minute guest, not an omnipresent ruler.

Bone Broth Unleashed: A Culinary Guide for Canine Wellness

Now, let's delve into the art and science of crafting bone broth tailor-made for our four-legged connoisseurs. As a culinary maestro for dogs, here are the fundamental principles and practical tips to ensure your bone broth creation is a masterpiece of health, safety, and irresistible flavors:

1. Pristine Ingredients Rule the Realm:
- Banish toxic temptations. Opt for natural, dog-safe ingredients, and steer clear of offenders like onions and excessive sodium.
- Ditch additives, embracing the purity that nature offers for the well-being of your discerning canine clientele.

2. The Raw Symphony of Bones:
- Engage the raw brilliance of bones with marrow—chicken, turkey, rabbit, beef, pork, or the regal oxtail.
- Raw bones, laden with nutrition, reign supreme over their cooked counterparts, safeguarding against splinters and potential choking hazards.

3. Herb and Spice Alchemy:
- Elevate the health quotient with the infusion of herbs and spices—turmeric, rosemary, thyme, and oregano stand as flavorful titans, and unleash anti-inflammatory prowess, fortifying your dog's immune system and overall vitality.

4. The Slow Symphony of Simmering:
- Let the bones and company waltz in a slow simmer, a culinary tango lasting at least 24 hours, and extract every ounce of nutrition and flavor from the bones, orchestrating a symphony that tantalizes the canine palate.

5. Strain for Purity:
- Filter the concoction through a fine-mesh strainer, bidding farewell to solids and potential hazards.
- Strive for a liquid elixir free from bone remnants and other culinary debris.

6. Freeze in Cubes, Unlocking Convenience:
- Cast your creation into the frozen embrace of ice cube trays, a symphony frozen in time for future delights, with each cube, a savory morsel, ready to thaw and grace your dog's bowl or other culinary creations.

7. Thawing Gracefully:
- When the moment to indulge arrives, gracefully thaw the frozen treasure. Extract desired cubes and place them in a dish.
- A gentle pour of hot water facilitates the thaw, transforming the frozen into a delectable addition to your dog's feast.

In conclusion, the symphony of crafting bone broth for dogs is not just a culinary pursuit but a wellness endeavor. With natural ingredients, herbs, a slow simmer, and strategic freezing, you weave a tapestry of health and taste for your loyal companion. May your culinary creations for dogs be nothing short of a gastronomic masterpiece!

Decoding Bone Broth Dosage: A Nutritional Compass for Your Canine Companion

How Much?

When it comes to introducing bone broth into your dog's diet, precision matters. According to expert advice:

- 1 Ounce per 10 Pounds:
  - A 10-pound dog can enjoy 2 ounces of bone broth split across two meals.
  - For a hefty 100-pound dog, the allowance extends to 20 ounces, divided into two servings per day.

Dosage Approach:

When introducing bone broth to your dog's diet, adopting a gradual and cautious approach is paramount. Dogs, like humans, can exhibit varied responses to new dietary additions. The goal is to initiate the introduction with a minimal amount and keenly observe your dog's reactions before making any significant adjustments.

A. Start Small:
- Commence with a small serving, perhaps a teaspoon or a tablespoon, depending on the size of your dog. This allows you to gauge their initial response without overwhelming their system.

B. Observation Phase:
- Pay close attention to how your dog reacts after consuming the bone broth. Look for signs of interest, enjoyment, or any immediate adverse reactions such as changes in behavior, digestive upset, or allergic responses.

C. Gradual Increase:
- Based on your observations, gradually increase the dosage over the next few days. This slow progression enables your dog's digestive system to adapt to the new addition, reducing the likelihood of any sudden adverse effects.

D. Monitor Behavior:
- Continue monitoring your dog's behavior, energy levels, and overall well-being as you increase the bone broth dosage. Positive responses, such as improved coat condition or increased vitality, can be indicators that the introduction is well-received.

E. Consult with Vet:
- If at any point you notice unusual or concerning reactions, consult with your veterinarian. They can provide guidance on adjusting the dosage or may recommend discontinuing the bone broth if necessary.

F. Individual Tolerance:
- Recognize that each dog is unique, and their tolerance levels may vary. Factors such as age, size, and overall health can influence how they respond to dietary changes.

G. Control the Schedule:
- Maintain a consistent feeding routine during this observation period. This allows you to associate any changes in your dog's behavior or health directly with the introduction of bone broth.

By proceeding in this careful manner, you not only prioritize your dog's well-being but also gain valuable insights into how bone broth integrates into their diet. Remember, patience and attentiveness are key components of this gradual introduction process.

Portion Control:
- Keep servings small to avoid overwhelming your dog. This ensures the experience remains enjoyable and not a digestive challenge.

Consult with the Vet:

Before you dive in, seek guidance from your veterinarian or a nutritionist to ensure the bone broth is nutritionally balanced and safe for your dog.

Too Much?

While bone broth offers health benefits, excess can pose risks:

1. Digestive Upset:
- Overconsumption may lead to digestive issues like vomiting and diarrhea.

2. Allergic Reactions:
- Some dogs might be allergic to ingredients like onions or garlic, causing adverse reactions.

3. Sodium Overload:
- High sodium content can be problematic, especially for dogs with kidney or heart conditions. To safeguard against sodium overload, these recipes are thoughtfully crafted. Dog-safe herbs and spices are incorporated for taste, ensuring a palatable experience without an overreliance on salt.

4. Nutrient Imbalance:
- Excessive intake may disrupt the nutritional balance if used as a substitute for a complete diet. The recipes presented in the next section of this Book are mainly full meals.

5. Choking Hazard:
- Bones can pose a choking risk, emphasizing the need for bone removal before serving.

In conclusion, moderation is key when incorporating bone broth into your dog's diet. Keep an eye on ingredients, portion sizes, and, if you notice any adverse reactions, consult your vet promptly. The goal is a healthy and balanced addition to your loyal companion's meals.

6

BONE BROTH: THE RECIPES
+ Two Alternatives

The Dog-Friendly Bone Broth Collection

Now, pay close attention, as we're about to delve into a selection of bone broth recipes that will have your four-legged friends drooling with anticipation. When crafting these recipes, remember, no toxic ingredients, and let's keep it natural, shall we? We're here to create something both delectable for us and safe for our furry companions.

1. Beefy Bliss Bone Broth:
Featuring the robust flavors of beef bones, carrots, celery, parsley, and water. It's not just a boost for your dog's diet; it's a symphony of nutrition that'll have your pooch doing happy spins at mealtime.

2. Instant Pot Delight for Dogs:
Utilizing beef marrow bones, pig's feet, celery, carrots, and parsley. This foolproof recipe guarantees a healthy bone broth tailored exclusively for your dog. Feel free to swap in chicken or turkey components, adding turkey necks or chicken feet for that extra gelatinous touch.

3. Mixed Bones Medley:
A blend of beef, chicken, and pork bones, combined with water, turmeric, and apple cider vinegar. This nutritional powerhouse supports your dog's joints, skin, coat, and digestion. Packed with protein, glycine, collagen, glutamine, and glucosamine – it's a health elixir in a bowl.

4. Slow Cooked Elegance:
Simple yet effective, with beef bones, apple cider vinegar, and water. An affordable way to whip up a canine delicacy. Use it as a meal topper, a nutrition enhancer, or as a special treat to pamper your furry friend.

5. Ginger & Parsley Infusion:
Featuring raw bones with marrow (chicken, turkey, rabbit, beef, pork, or oxtail), ginger root, parsley, and water. A nutrient-packed, superfood extravaganza for your dog. Loaded with easily absorbable, hydrating nutrients, it's the ultimate building block for your dog's well-being.

6. Chicken Bone Broth:
Our Canine Comfort Chicken Bone Broth is a nourishing elixir crafted with the finest ingredients – tender chicken bones, aromatic vegetables, and a dash of love. Simmered to perfection for 24 hours, this broth not only adds a burst of flavor to your dog's meals but also brings a wealth of nutrients, promoting joint health, a lustrous coat, and overall well-being with every sip.

7. Mushroom Broth:
Our Mushroom Broth is a delectable blend of shiitake, portobello, and crimini mushrooms, sautéed to perfection and simmered for 20 minutes to create a flavorful elixir that adds both taste and nutrition to your dog's diet.

8. Vegetable Broth:
Crafted with care, our Vegetable Broth for dogs is a harmonious blend of carrots, celery, onion, and garlic, sautéed in olive oil and simmered for 2-3 hours. This delightful concoction ensures a nutritious and dog-safe addition to your pup's diet, free from harmful additives and bursting with garden-fresh goodness.

Crafting the Perfect Beef Bone Broth for Your Pooch

Now, let's dive into the culinary realm of crafting a beef bone broth that'll have your dog's tail wagging with joy. This recipe is not just a meal; it's a nutritional powerhouse packed with flavors that will leave your furry friend craving for more.

Ingredients:
- 4-5 pounds of beef marrow bones
- 1 large carrot, chopped
- 1 celery stalk, chopped
- 1/2 cup parsley leaves
- 2 tablespoons apple cider vinegar
- 12 cups of water

Instructions:

1. Preheat and Roast:
   - Kick things off by preheating your oven to 400°F. Lay out those beef marrow bones on a baking sheet and let them roast in the oven for a tantalizing 30 minutes.

2. Slow Cooker Magic:
   - Transfer those beautifully roasted bones into the spacious embrace of a large slow cooker. Add in the chopped carrot, celery, parsley leaves, apple cider vinegar, and water.

3. Low and Slow:
   - Cover the slow cooker, set it on low heat, and let the magic happen over the next 24 hours.

4. Cool and Strain:
   - After a day of simmering goodness, turn off the slow cooker and let the broth cool. Once it's at a comfortable temperature, strain it through a fine-mesh strainer, bidding farewell to the solids.

5. Freeze for Future Delight:
   - Pour this liquid gold into ice cube trays and freeze them for future culinary adventures.

To Serve:
   - Thaw the frozen bone broth cubes by placing your desired amount in a dish. A touch of hot water will do the trick. Once thawed, let the feast begin – whether it's enhancing your dog's meal or serving it as a delectable treat.

This Beef Bone Broth for Dogs is not just a recipe; it's a commitment to your dog's well-being. Nutritious, easy to make, and with the added convenience of freezing for future indulgence, it's a culinary delight your dog will thank you for.

BEEF BROTH RECIPE

Whipping Up Instant Pot Magic for Your Pup's Delight

Now, let's embark on a culinary journey with the Instant Pot, crafting a bone broth that will have your dog's taste buds doing a happy dance. This recipe is not just about convenience; it's a burst of flavors and nutrition that your furry friend will devour with enthusiasm.

Ingredients:
- 2 pounds beef marrow bones
- 2 pig's feet
- 1 large carrot, chopped
- 1 celery stalk, chopped
- 1/2 cup parsley leaves
- 2 tablespoons apple cider vinegar
- 12 cups of water

Instructions:

1. Pot of Plenty:
   - Load up your Instant Pot with the beef marrow bones, pig's feet, chopped carrot, celery, parsley leaves, apple cider vinegar, and water.

2. Seal and Cook:
   - Lock in the goodness by closing the Instant Pot lid and setting the valve to 'sealing.' Cook on high pressure for 3 hours.

3. Natural Unveiling:
   - Allow the Instant Pot to release pressure naturally for 30 minutes, letting the flavors reach their full potential.

4. Cool and Strain:
   - Once the pressure's off, crack open the Instant Pot and let the broth cool for a few hours. Afterward, strain it through a fine-mesh strainer, bidding farewell to any remnants.

5. Freeze for Future Feasts:
   - Pour this liquid gold into ice cube trays and freeze them for upcoming canine feasts.

To Serve:
   - Thaw the frozen bone broth cubes by placing your desired amount in a dish. A splash of hot water will do the trick. Once thawed, whether enhancing your dog's meal or serving as a delightful treat, the options are as endless as the joy it brings.

This Instant Pot Bone Broth for Dogs is more than a recipe; it's a culinary innovation. Nutritious, freezer-friendly, and a burst of flavor for your pup's palate – it's a canine delight waiting to be savored.

Crafting Canine Culinary Excellence:
Mixed Bones Bone Broth

Now, let's delve into the art of blending flavors and nutrients with our Mixed Bones Bone Broth for Dogs. This recipe isn't just about concocting a broth; it's a symphony of mixed bones, herbs, and spices that will have your dog's tail wagging in delight.

Ingredients:
- 3 pounds mixed bones (beef, chicken, pork)
- 12 cups of water
- 1/2 teaspoon turmeric powder
- 1/4 teaspoon Italian herbs (sage, rosemary, thyme, oregano, basil)
- 2 tablespoons lemon juice

Instructions:

1. Diverse Mix in the Pot:
   - Combine the mixed bones, water, turmeric powder, Italian herbs, and lemon juice in a large pot.

2. Bring to Life:
   - Let the flavors mingle as you bring the mixture to a boil over high heat.

3. Gentle Simmer:
   - Reduce the heat to low, allowing it to simmer for a glorious 24 hours. Patience is the key to this nutrient-rich elixir.

4. Cool and Strain:
   - Once the magic has happened, turn off the heat and let the broth cool for a few hours. Strain it through a fine-mesh strainer, bidding farewell to any remnants.

5. Freeze for Future Feasts:
   - Transform this liquid gold into ice cube trays and freeze them, ready for future feasts.

To Serve:
   - Thaw the frozen bone broth cubes by placing your desired amount in a dish. A splash of hot water will do the trick. Once thawed, whether enhancing your dog's meal or serving as a delightful treat, the options are as endless as the joy it brings.

This Mixed Bones Bone Broth for Dogs isn't merely a culinary creation; it's a testament to the art of crafting nourishment with flair. Beyond the realms of a traditional recipe, it emerges as a true canine delight, weaving together a symphony of flavors and nutritional richness that elevates your dog's dining experience.

Embarking on a Culinary Journey:
   - Each sip of this bone broth unveils a masterful blend of diverse bones, harmonizing beef, chicken, and pork, infused with the warmth of turmeric, aromatic Italian herbs, and a dash of bright lemon juice.

MIXED BONES BROTH RECIPE

A Symphony of Nutrition and Taste:
- This concoction isn't just about meeting dietary needs; it's a celebration of health and flavor. The variety of bones contributes to a spectrum of nutrients, from protein and collagen to essential vitamins and minerals, fortifying your dog's well-being with each indulgent slurp.

Versatility in a Cube:
- Freeze this liquid treasure in ice cube trays, creating bite-sized nuggets of canine joy. Whether enhancing a daily meal or serving as an occasional treat, the versatility of this bone broth transcends mere sustenance.

A Delectable Conclusion:
- In conclusion, this Mixed Bones Bone Broth for Dogs isn't just a recipe on paper. It's a culinary journey, a symphony of taste, and a nutritional masterpiece. With each sip, your dog indulges in a delicacy crafted with care, making mealtime an experience that transcends the ordinary.

Why we Simmer:
The purpose of the gentle simmer in this recipe goes beyond mere cooking; it's the alchemy that transforms a pot of ingredients into a rich elixir for your canine companion. Let's delve into the significance of this gentle simmer in creating the Mixed Bones Bone Broth for Dogs:

1. Nutrient Extraction: The slow, gentle simmer allows the bones to release their nutritional essence gradually. This process coaxes out essential nutrients, including collagen, amino acids, and minerals, infusing the broth with a powerhouse of elements vital for your dog's joint health, coat, and overall well-being.

2. Flavor Fusion: The gentle simmer serves as a patient maestro, orchestrating the marriage of diverse bones, herbs, and spices. It allows the flavors to meld and dance together, creating a symphony that's not just palatable but a true delight for your dog's discerning taste buds.

3. Gelatin Production: The extended simmer encourages the production of gelatin from the bones. Gelatin is a key component that adds a velvety texture to the broth, contributing to its richness and providing additional benefits for joint health and digestion.

4. Release of Aromatics: Herbs, spices, and other aromatic elements reach their full potential during a gentle simmer. The prolonged heat coaxes out their essential oils and flavors, infusing the broth with a fragrant profile that elevates the overall sensory experience for your dog.

5. Tenderness and Safety: Slow and steady wins the race when it comes to bone broth. A gentle simmer prevents the rapid boiling that could lead to overcooking or harsh temperatures that might compromise the nutritional integrity of the ingredients. It ensures a tender and safe extraction of goodness from the bones.

In essence, the gentle simmer in this recipe is the maestro's wand, conducting a culinary symphony where every note, every flavor, and every nutrient is coaxed out with care and precision. It transforms a pot of ingredients into a potion that transcends the ordinary, providing your dog with a delectable and nutritious elixir crafted with culinary finesse.

Slow Cooker Elegance: Bone Broth for Dogs

The Slow Cooker Bone Broth for Dogs is a labor of love, a 24-hour symphony of nourishment that delicately extracts the essence of beef bones, lemon slices, and a blend of aromatic herbs. As this elixir simmers with patience, it transforms into a rich, collagen-packed concoction that serves as a testament to culinary craftsmanship. The infusion of turmeric, dried rosemary, thyme, and oregano adds not just flavor but a fragrant symphony of aromas, promoting anti-inflammatory benefits for your dog's immune system and overall well-being. With a slow-cooked tenderness that ensures nutrient integrity, this bone broth, frozen into convenient cubes, becomes a versatile and nutritious addition to your dog's meals or a delightful treat—a culinary masterpiece designed to elevate your furry friend's health and dining experience.

Ingredients:
- 4-5 pounds beef bones
- 12 cups of water
- 1 lemon, sliced
- 1 teaspoon turmeric powder
- 1/2 teaspoon dried rosemary
- 1/2 teaspoon dried thyme
- 1/2 teaspoon dried oregano

Instructions:
1. Add the beef bones, water, lemon slices, turmeric powder, dried rosemary, dried thyme, and dried oregano to a slow cooker.
2. Cover and let the slow cooker work its magic on low heat for 24 hours.
3. After this slow infusion, turn off the cooker and let the broth cool for a few hours.
4. Once cooled, strain the liquid gold through a fine-mesh strainer, bidding farewell to the solids.
5. Pour this elixir into ice cube trays, freezing it for future moments of delight.

To serve:
When the canine craving strikes, retrieve the desired cubes from the freezer. A dash of hot water will gracefully thaw this nutritious treat. Whether blended with your dog's meal or offered as a standalone delight, this Slow Cooker Bone Broth is a culinary blessing.

To Slow Cook or InstaPot?

In the realm of bone broth for dogs, the Slow Cooker variation stands as a distinct symphony, each note played deliberately and tenderly. Let's explore how this rendition differs from its Instant Pot counterpart, offering a unique canine culinary experience.

Slow Cooker Elegance:
1. Time-Honored Infusion: Unlike the swift pace of the Instant Pot, the Slow Cooker takes its time—a patient 24 hours of low heat. This unhurried process allows for a gentle extraction of nutrients, creating a broth enriched with collagen, amino acids, and minerals, a true elixir for your dog's vitality.

2. Aromatic Bouquet: The Slow Cooker accentuates the aromatic dance of herbs. Dried rosemary, thyme, and oregano slowly release their essential oils, infusing the broth with a fragrant profile that elevates not only the flavor but also the olfactory joy for your discerning dog.

3. Tender Love and Care: This method embraces the philosophy of "slow and steady." A gentle simmer prevents overcooking, ensuring the nutritional integrity of the ingredients remains intact. It results in a tender extraction of goodness from the bones, offering both safety and nutrition.

Instant Pot Boldness:
1. Swift Symphony: The Instant Pot, with its high-pressure prowess, condenses the symphony into a 3-hour crescendo. It's the rock concert compared to the Slow Cooker's classical performance, producing a bone broth that's efficiently nutritious for your dog.

2. Efficiency Unleashed: The Instant Pot doesn't dabble in subtleties; it's a powerhouse of efficiency. Ideal for pet parents with a tight schedule, it delivers a quick yet nutrient-rich broth without compromising on health benefits.

3. Adaptability: The Instant Pot variation offers versatility in meat choices. Whether beef, chicken, or turkey, you can tailor the bones to suit your dog's preferences, ensuring a diverse nutritional profile.

In essence, the Slow Cooker Bone Broth is a gentle ballad, allowing each ingredient to express itself fully, while the Instant Pot variation is a lively concert, delivering a bold and efficient performance. Both, however, share the same goal—a nutritious and flavorful elixir for your canine companion. The choice depends on your preferred tempo in the canine culinary orchestra.

Ginger and Parsley Infusion: A Bone Broth for Dogs

The Ginger and Parsley Bone Broth for Dogs is a culinary marvel that combines the richness of raw bones with the zesty warmth of ginger and the vibrant freshness of parsley. Slow-cooked for 24 hours, this broth becomes a nutritional powerhouse, brimming with collagen, amino acids, and minerals essential for your dog's well-being. The addition of ginger and parsley, both known for their anti-inflammatory properties, elevates this elixir to not just a treat but a health-boosting concoction. The versatility of this recipe shines through with optional variations, including the anti-inflammatory turmeric or a touch of apple cider vinegar for enhanced mineral extraction. Frozen into convenient cubes, this bone broth becomes a convenient addition to your dog's meals, offering benefits for digestion, joint health, and immune support—a testament to the blend of science and culinary finesse in canine nutrition.

Ingredients:
- 3-4 pounds raw bones with marrow (chicken, turkey, rabbit, beef, pork, or oxtail)
- 3 inches ginger root, sliced
- 2 ounces parsley, chopped
- 12 cups of water

Instructions:
1. Add the raw bones with marrow, sliced ginger root, chopped parsley, and water to a slow cooker.
2. Cover the slow cooker and cook on low heat for 24 hours.
3. After 24 hours, turn off the slow cooker and let the broth cool for a few hours.
4. Once cooled, strain the broth through a fine-mesh strainer and discard the solids.
5. Pour the broth into ice cube trays and freeze for future use.

Variations:
1. Add turmeric powder to the broth for its anti-inflammatory properties.
2. Add a small amount of apple cider vinegar instead of lemon juice to help extract the minerals from the bones.

To thaw the frozen bone broth, remove the desired amount of cubes from the freezer and place them in a dish. Pour over a little hot water to thaw it. Once it's thawed, you can add it to your dog's food or serve it as a treat.

In conclusion, this recipe for Ginger and Parsley Bone Broth for Dogs is easy to make, nutritious, and safe for dogs. You can freeze it in ice cube trays for future use and thaw it by adding hot water. Ginger and parsley have anti-inflammatory properties that can help support your dog's immune system and overall health. This bone broth recipe is a great addition to your dog's current diet, as it encourages a healthy gut, improves digestion, strengthens joints, and reinforces your dog's immune system.

GINGER & PARSLEY BONE BROTH RECIPE

Chicken Bone Broth for Canine Delight

This Chicken Bone Broth for Canine Delight is more than a recipe; it's a symphony of flavors and nutrients crafted with your dog's well-being in mind. The slow infusion of raw chicken bones, coupled with aromatic vegetables and herbs, creates a broth that not only entices your dog's palate but also nourishes from the inside out. It's a culinary masterpiece, simmered to perfection, offering your furry friend a wholesome and delectable addition to their meals. Whether served as a treat or poured over regular meals, this chicken bone broth elevates your dog's dining experience to a whole new level of delight.

Ingredients:
- 4-5 pounds of raw chicken bones with marrow
- 1 large carrot, roughly chopped
- 1 celery stalk, roughly chopped
- 1/2 cup parsley leaves
- 2 tablespoons apple cider vinegar
- 12 cups of water

Instructions:
1. Begin by sourcing quality raw chicken bones with marrow, ensuring they're free from cooked bones that can splinter.

2. In a roasting pan, arrange the chicken bones and roast them in the oven at 400°F for 30 minutes. This step enhances the flavor profile of your broth.

3. Transfer the roasted bones to your trusty slow cooker, adding in the chopped carrot, celery, parsley leaves, apple cider vinegar, and water.

4. Set the slow cooker to low heat and let the magic happen over the next 24 hours. This slow infusion extracts the rich nutrients from the bones, creating a broth that's not only tasty but also packed with goodness.

5. Once the slow cooker has worked its wonders, turn it off and allow the broth to cool. Patience is key; good things come to those who wait.

6. Strain the broth through a fine-mesh strainer, bidding farewell to the solids. What remains is a liquid gold that will soon grace your dog's bowl.

7. For convenient storage, pour the broth into ice cube trays and freeze, ready to be served in convenient portions.

Mushroom Melody Broth: A Canine Symphony of Flavor and Nutrition

The Dog-Safe Mushroom Broth is a delightful departure from traditional bone broths, offering a vegetarian twist to pamper your pup's palate. While it's essential to consult with your veterinarian before contemplating a vegetarian diet for your pet, this mushroom broth serves as a tasty variation or occasional treat. Crafted with an array of mushrooms like shiitake, portobello, and crimini, this broth is a burst of flavor and nutrition. The sautéed mushrooms in butter bring a rich, earthy essence, while optional additions of shredded turmeric and ginger roots provide a zesty kick and potential anti-inflammatory benefits. Simmered to perfection, the broth is then pureed for a velvety texture, ready to be served as a standalone treat or conveniently frozen for later indulgence. It's a culinary departure that caters to both taste buds and health-conscious pet parenting. The caveat being: never allow your dog to eat mushrooms in the wild.

Notes on this recipe:

Dogs may have different preferences when it comes to mushrooms, and individual reactions can vary. While some dogs might enjoy the taste and texture of mushrooms, others may not show much interest. However, it's essential to note that not all mushrooms are safe for dogs.

Certain varieties of mushrooms, like shiitake, portobello, and crimini, can be used in small amounts to create a flavorful and nutritious broth. Mushrooms offer various nutrients and can provide benefits such as immune support and anti-inflammatory properties. However, it's crucial to consult with a veterinarian before introducing mushrooms or any new ingredient into your dog's diet to ensure it aligns with their specific health needs and dietary requirements. Additionally, some dogs may be allergic to certain mushrooms, so observing their reaction and introducing mushrooms gradually is advisable. Here is a recipe for mushroom broth for dogs:

Ingredients:

- 1 cup of culinary-grade, human-safe, cultivated mushrooms, chopped
- 2 cups of water
- 1 tablespoon of butter
- Shredded turmeric root (optional)
- Shredded ginger root (optional)

Instructions:

1. Saute the chopped mushrooms in butter until they are soft.
2. Add 2 cups of water and simmer for 20 minutes.
3. Add shredded turmeric root and ginger root (optional).
4. Puree the ingredients and serve (or freeze for later).

Canine Nourishment in a Bowl: Vegetable Broth

Crafted with a culinary conscience for our four-legged companions, the Canine Vegetable Broth is a savory addition to a dog-centric diet. This broth, a flavorful medley of carrots, celery, onion, and garlic sautéed to perfection in olive oil, is a testament to the commitment to your dog's well-being. The patient simmer of 2-3 hours extracts the essence of each ingredient, creating a wholesome elixir that not only enhances your dog's meals but also delivers a burst of nutrients. Freeze it in ice cube trays for convenience, and thaw it when needed for a delightful addition to your dog's culinary experience. Remember, while dogs relish the flavors of this vegetable broth, they are not vegetarians, and this recipe is designed to complement their omnivorous diet.

Ingredients:

- 2 carrots, chopped
- 2 celery stalks, chopped
- 1 onion, chopped
- 2 garlic cloves, chopped
- 1 tablespoon of olive oil
- 12 cups of water

Instructions:

1. Begin by sautéing the chopped carrots, celery, onion, and garlic in olive oil until they reach a delightful softness.
2. Add 12 cups of water to the mix and bring it to a gentle boil.
3. Reduce the heat, allowing the concoction to simmer for 2-3 hours. This patient simmering extracts the essence of each ingredient, creating a broth bursting with flavors and nutrients.
4. Strain the broth through a fine-mesh strainer, bidding farewell to the solids, and retaining the liquid gold.
5. For convenient serving, pour the broth into ice cube trays and freeze, ready to grace your dog's bowl.

Thawing Instructions:
To thaw the frozen broth, extract the desired number of cubes and place them in a dish. A gentle pour of hot water is all it takes to thaw this canine elixir. Once unfrozen, it's ready to complement your dog's meals or serve as a delightful treat.

7

52
DOG-SAFE MEALS
&
INGREDIENTS
RELATED TO SAME

Paws and Palates Unleashed

Get ready for a culinary odyssey like no other, where each week brings forth a
sensational new creation for your furry friend!

We're diving headfirst into a feast of 52 meticulously crafted, dog-safe meals, each a
gastronomic triumph designed to make your pup's taste buds do the happy dance.
From succulent bone broths that could rival any Michelin-starred dish to hearty stews
that redefine canine comfort food, we're taking dog dining to a whole new level of
excellence. Join us on this year-long adventure, where every meal isn't just a culinary
delight for your pooch but a celebration of their health, happiness, and the joy they
bring to your home.

Let the tail-wagging commence!

1

Ground Beef and Sweet Potato Extravaganza

When it comes to culinary prowess for your four-legged friend, this recipe takes the lead, combining the nutritional powerhouse of sweet potatoes with the savory punch of ground beef. Sweet potatoes, a canine superfood, bring a riot of vitamins A, B6, C, and an array of essential minerals, ensuring your dog's skin, coat, eyes, nerves, and muscles are in top-notch condition. Now, let's talk beef – a protein-packed hero in this dish, offering a nutrient-rich blend of iron, zinc, and vitamin B12. Yet, it's a balancing act; watch out for the fat content, opt for lean beef, and ensure thorough cooking to dodge any health hiccups. This gastronomic marvel promises variety, nutrition, and a tail-wagging good time, perfect for your discerning pooch. It's a canine feast fit for a king, or should I say, a king-sized appetite!

The Sweet Potato:
It is hard to go wrong with a Sweet Potato. Properly cooked sweet potatoes are high in fiber, which helps with your dog's digestion. They are a great source of vitamin A, which promotes healthy skin, coat, eyes, nerves, and muscles. They are are also high in vitamin B6 and vitamin C, as well as calcium, potassium, dietary fiber, antioxidants, and iron. Finally, they are low in fat, making them a healthy treat for your dog.

Beef:
Benefits of Ground Beef for Dogs
- High in protein: Ground beef is a good source of protein, which is essential for building and repairing muscles, tissues, and cells in dogs.
- Nutrient-dense: Ground beef is high in nutrients that dogs need, such as iron, zinc, and vitamin B12.
- Omega-3 fatty acids: Ground beef contains omega-3 fatty acids, which can help improve skin health and boost the immune system in dogs.
- Variety: Adding ground beef to your dog's diet can provide variety and make meal time more interesting for your dog.

Limitations of Ground Beef for Dogs
- Fat content: Ground beef can be high in fat, which can cause digestive upset and obesity in dogs if consumed in large amounts.
- Saturated fat: Ground beef contains saturated fat, which is not the best type of fat for dogs to consume.
- Cost: Ground beef can be expensive, so it may not be a practical option for some dog owners.
- Preparation: Ground beef should be cooked thoroughly to avoid the risk of bacterial contamination and foodborne illness.
- It is also essential to be on the look-out for allergies to beef in regards to your dog.

Ground beef can be a nutritious addition to your dog's diet, but it should be fed in moderation and prepared properly to avoid any potential health risks. It's important to

choose lean ground beef and avoid high-fat options, and to consult with your veterinarian if you have any concerns about your dog's health or dietary needs.
Her we go:

Ingredients

- 1 pound ground beef, cooked
- 2 cups sweet potatoes, cooked and mashed
- 1 cup green beans, cooked and chopped
- 1 tablespoon olive oil
- 1 teaspoon dried parsley

Instructions

1. Cook the ground beef in a large skillet until browned and fully cooked.
2. In a separate pot, cook the sweet potatoes until they are soft enough to mash.
3. Cook the green beans in boiling water for about 5 minutes, then chop them into small pieces.
4. In a large mixing bowl, combine the cooked ground beef, mashed sweet potatoes, and chopped green beans.
5. Add the olive oil and dried parsley to the mixing bowl and mix everything together until it is well combined.
6. Let the mixture cool before serving it to your dog.

This recipe is nutritionally complete and balanced, and it yields approximately 4 cups of food, equating to 1,200 calories (Kcals), which is enough servings of food for one day for a 40 lb dog to maintain weight. It is also easy to make and a fan favorite, making it best for dogs with sensitive stomachs or those who are picky eaters.

Chicken and Rice with Carrots

Indulge your pup in the delectable symphony of flavors with our Chicken and Rice with Carrots recipe – a canine culinary masterpiece designed to tantalize taste buds and nourish from within. Tender chicken, wholesome rice, and vibrant carrots come together in a delightful fusion that not only satisfies your dog's palate but also provides a wholesome balance of nutrients. This savory creation ensures a tail-wagging, paw-licking experience, offering a wholesome feast that speaks volumes about your commitment to your furry companion's well-being.

Ingredients

- 7 ounces chicken, cooked and shredded
- 1 cup cooked brown rice
- 1 cup cooked carrots, mashed or finely chopped
- 1 tablespoon olive oil

Optional Additions

- 1/4 cup cooked peas
- 1/4 cup cooked green beans
- 1/4 cup cooked sweet potatoes, mashed or finely chopped

Instructions

1. In a large skillet, heat the olive oil over medium heat.
2. Add the cooked chicken to the skillet and cook for 5-7 minutes, stirring occasionally, until heated through.
3. Add the cooked brown rice and carrots to the skillet and stir to combine with the chicken.
4. If using, add the cooked peas, green beans, and sweet potatoes to the skillet and stir to combine.
5. Cook the mixture for an additional 2-3 minutes, until all the ingredients are well combined and heated through.
6. Remove the skillet from the heat and let the mixture cool before serving it to your dog.

Freezing and Storing
This recipe can be stored in an airtight container in the refrigerator for up to three days. You can also freeze it in individual portions for longer storage. Before serving any frozen portions, make sure to thaw them in the refrigerator overnight. Always consult with your veterinarian before making any changes to your dog's diet.

Carrots

Carrots are a nutritious and healthy food option for dogs. Here are some benefits of feeding carrots to your dog:

1. Vitamin A
Carrots are rich in Vitamin A, which is essential for maintaining good eye health in dogs.

2. Low calorie
Carrots are low in calories and can serve as a healthy, low-calorie snack for your dog.

3. Fiber
Carrots are a good source of fiber, which can help improve your dog's digestive system and prevent constipation.

4. Nutrient-dense
Carrots are high in nutrients that dogs need, such as iron, zinc, and vitamin B6.

5. Dental health
Chewing on carrots can help improve your dog's dental health by removing plaque and promoting healthy teeth and gums.

However, there are some limitations to feeding carrots to your dog. For example, carrots can be difficult for dogs to digest, so it's important to cook them before feeding them to your dog. Additionally, carrots should be fed in moderation and cut into small pieces to prevent choking, especially in small dogs. It's also important to consult with your veterinarian before introducing any new foods to your dog's diet, especially if your dog has any specific dietary needs or health conditions.

3

Turkey and Pumpkin Bowl

This turkey and pumpkin bowl is a healthy and tasty meal for your dog. It is made with simple, wholesome ingredients that are free from any harmful additives or preservatives. Remember to always check with your veterinarian before introducing any new foods to your dog's diet, and to feed this bowl in moderation as part of a balanced diet.

Ingredients

- 1 pound ground turkey
- 1 cup pumpkin puree
- 1 cup cooked brown rice
- 1 cup cooked sweet potato, mashed
- 1/2 cup green beans, chopped
- 1/2 cup carrots, chopped
- 1/4 cup fresh parsley, chopped
- 1 tablespoon olive oil

Instructions

1. Preheat the oven to 350°F.
2. In a large mixing bowl, combine the ground turkey, pumpkin puree, cooked brown rice, mashed sweet potato, chopped green beans, chopped carrots, and chopped parsley.
3. Mix well until all ingredients are evenly distributed.
4. Grease a baking dish with olive oil and transfer the mixture to the dish.
5. Bake for 30-35 minutes, or until the turkey is cooked through and the vegetables are tender.
6. Let the mixture cool completely before serving to your dog.

Freezing and Thawing

To freeze the stew, let it cool completely and then transfer it to an airtight container or freezer-safe zip-top bag. Label the container or bag with the date and contents, and store it in the freezer for up to three months. To thaw the stew, place it in the refrigerator overnight. Once thawed, reheat on the stove before serving it to your dog. The stew can be stored in the refrigerator for up to three days.

4

Beef and Broccoli Stir Fry

Succulent beef, crisp broccoli, and a medley of dog-friendly ingredients come together to create a symphony of flavors and textures. This dish is more than just a treat; it's a nutrient-packed ensemble, providing your dog with essential protein for muscle health, vitamins for overall well-being, and a burst of fiber for digestive vitality.

Ingredients

- 1 pound ground beef, cooked
- 2 cups broccoli florets, cooked and chopped
- 1 cup cooked brown rice
- 1 tablespoon olive oil
- 1 teaspoon dried ginger

Optional Additions

- 1/4 cup cooked carrots, chopped
- 1/4 cup cooked green beans, chopped

Instructions

1. In a large skillet, heat the olive oil over medium heat.
2. Add the cooked ground beef to the skillet and cook for 5-7 minutes, stirring occasionally, until heated through.
3. Add the cooked broccoli florets, brown rice, and dried ginger to the skillet and stir to combine with the beef.
4. If using, add the cooked carrots and green beans to the skillet and stir to combine.
5. Cook the mixture for an additional 2-3 minutes, until all the ingredients are well combined and heated through.
6. Remove the skillet from the heat and let the mixture cool before serving it to your dog.

Freezing and Thawing

To freeze the stir fry, let it cool completely and then transfer it to an airtight container or freezer-safe zip-top bag. Label the container or bag with the date and contents, and store it in the freezer for up to three months. To thaw the stir fry, place it in the refrigerator overnight. Once thawed, you can reheat it in the microwave or on the stove before serving it to your dog. The stir fry can be stored in the refrigerator for up to three days.

Olive Oil

While olive oil is generally considered safe for dogs in moderation and can even offer certain health benefits, excessive consumption can lead to digestive upset. Dogs may experience symptoms such as diarrhea, vomiting, or abdominal discomfort if they ingest too much olive oil.

Olive oil is high in fat, and introducing large amounts of fat into a dog's diet abruptly can overwhelm their digestive system. It's crucial to incorporate any dietary changes gradually and monitor your dog's response. If you suspect that your dog has consumed an excessive amount of olive oil and is exhibiting signs of digestive upset, it's advisable to consult with a veterinarian for guidance tailored to your pet's specific situation.

Benefits Include:

Healthy fats: Olive oil contains healthy monounsaturated fats that can help break down fat cells and lower cholesterol in dogs.

Skin and coat health: Olive oil contains phytonutrients, vitamin E, and omega-3 fatty acids that can help keep your dog's skin moisturized and well-nourished, adding shine and strength to their hair.

Antioxidants: Olive oil contains antioxidants, such as vitamin E, that can help protect your dog's cell membranes from free radical damage and promote overall health.

There are some limitations to feeding olive oil to your dog:

Digestive upset: Olive oil can cause digestive upset in dogs if consumed in large amounts or if the dog has a sensitive stomach.

Greasy skin: Too much olive oil can make your dog's skin greasy and provide a breeding ground for yeast and bacteria.

Cost: Olive oil can be expensive, so it may not be a practical option for some dog owners.

Preparation: Olive oil should be added to your dog's food in small amounts and not applied directly to their coat, as they may lick it off and counteract the benefits.

5

Chicken and Spinach Stew with Almond Crackers

This culinary masterpiece, the Chicken and Spinach Delight, is not just a meal for your dog; it's a symphony of flavors and nutrition that will have their tails wagging in delight. Crafted to perfection, this recipe provides a nutritionally complete and balanced experience, yielding approximately 4 cups of tantalizing goodness, equivalent to 1,200 calories (Kcals). It's not just a meal; it's an experience tailored for the refined palate of your four-legged companion, especially ideal for those with sensitive stomachs or picky eaters.

And now, let's talk about the Almond Crackers – a crowning glory to this dish. Crush them over this creation, or save them for delightful snacks and treats. It's a culinary journey that goes beyond the ordinary, offering a combination of health and taste that your dog truly deserves.

Ingredients

- 1 pound boneless, skinless chicken breasts, cooked and shredded
- 2 cups fresh spinach, finely chopped
- 1 cup cooked brown rice
- 1 tablespoon olive oil
- 1 teaspoon dried oregano

Optional Addition

- 1/4 cup cooked carrots, finely chopped
- 1/4 cup cooked sweet potatoes, mashed or finely chopped

Instructions

1. In a generous skillet, heat the olive oil over medium heat, setting the stage for culinary excellence.
2. Introduce the cooked and shredded chicken to the skillet, orchestrating a sizzling performance for 5-7 minutes until it reaches a crescendo of perfection.
3. Cue the entrance of the chopped spinach, brown rice, and dried oregano, harmonizing with the chicken in a delightful melody of flavors.
4. For those opting for an encore, add the cooked carrots and sweet potatoes, creating a symphony of colors and textures.
5. Let this culinary composition play for an additional 2-3 minutes until the ingredients are perfectly in tune.
6. Conclude this gastronomic masterpiece by allowing it to cool before serving it to your appreciative audience – your beloved dog.

6

Almond Crackers

These almond crackers are a healthy and tasty treat for your dog. They are made with only a few simple ingredients and are free from any harmful additives or preservatives. Remember to always check with your veterinarian before introducing any new foods to your dog's diet, and to feed these crackers in moderation as part of a balanced diet.

Ingredients
- 2 cups almond flour
- 1/2 teaspoon salt
- 1/4 cup water
- 2 tablespoons olive oi

Instructions
1. Preheat the oven to 350°F.
2. In a large mixing bowl, combine the almond flour and salt.
3. Add the water and olive oil to the bowl and mix until a dough forms.
4. Roll out the dough on a piece of parchment paper until it is about 1/8 inch thick.
5. Use a cookie cutter or knife to cut the dough into small cracker shapes.
6. Place the crackers on a baking sheet lined with parchment paper.
7. Bake for 10-12 minutes, or until the crackers are golden brown and crispy.
8. Let the crackers cool completely before serving to your dog.

Almonds

Benefits:

High in nutrients

Almonds are rich in nutrients, such as vitamin E, magnesium, and phosphorus, which can help support your dog's overall health and well-being.

Healthy fats

Almonds contain healthy mono-unsaturated fats that can help break down fat cells and lower cholesterol in dogs

Limitations:

Digestive upset

Almonds can cause digestive upset in dogs if consumed in large amounts or if the dog has a sensitive stomach

Turkey and Carrot Mash with Cinnamon Sprinkle

This recipe is nutritionally complete and balanced, and it yields approximately 4 cups of food, equating to 1,200 calories (Kcals), which is enough servings of food for one day for a 40 lb dog to maintain weight. It is also easy to make and a fan favorite, making it best for dogs with sensitive stomachs or those who are picky eaters.

Ingredients:
- 1 pound ground turkey, cooked
- 2 cups carrots, cooked and mashed
- 1 tablespoon olive oil
- 1 teaspoon dried rosemary
- 1 pinch of Cinnamon

Optional Additions

- 1/4 cup cooked green beans, chopped
- 1/4 cup cooked sweet potatoes, mashed or finely chopped

Instructions
1. In a large skillet, heat the olive oil over medium heat.
2. Add the cooked ground turkey to the skillet and cook for 5-7 minutes, stirring occasionally, until heated through.
3. Add the mashed carrots and dried rosemary to the skillet and stir to combine with the turkey.
4. If using, add the cooked green beans and sweet potatoes to the skillet and stir to combine.
5. Cook the mixture for an additional 2-3 minutes, until all the ingredients are well combined and heated through.
6. Remove the skillet from the heat and let the mixture cool before serving it to your dog.

Cinnamon

In small amounts, cinnamon is safe and healthy for dogs. It can help support brain function, improve focus and memory, and also has anti-inflammatory properties.

8

Beef and Cauliflower Mash with Pumpkin Dollop

This might seem like an odd combination but Cauliflower and Pumpkin go great together.

Ingredients
- 1 pound ground beef
- 1 small head of cauliflower, cut into florets
- 1 cup frozen peas
- 1 tablespoon olive oil
- a dollop of puréd pumpkin to top

Instructions
1. In a large skillet, cook the ground beef over medium heat until browned and cooked through. Remove from the skillet and set aside.
2. In the same skillet, add the olive oil and cauliflower florets. Cook for 5-7 minutes, or until the cauliflower is tender.
3. In a separate pot, cook the frozen peas according to the package instructions. Drain and set aside.
4. In a food processor or blender, combine the cooked cauliflower and ground beef. Pulse until the mixture is well combined and has a mashed potato-like consistency.
5. Stir in the cooked peas.
6. Allow the mixture to cool before serving to your dog. Store any leftovers in an airtight container in the refrigerator for up to 3 days.

Freezing and Thawing
To freeze the Beef and Cauliflower Mash, divide the mixture into individual serving sizes and place them in airtight freezer-safe containers or resealable bags. Label the containers with the date and freeze for up to 3 months.

To thaw, simply remove a portion from the freezer and place it in the refrigerator overnight. Once thawed, you can reheat the mixture in the microwave for 15-30 seconds before serving to your dog.

Add the pumpkin when serving.

PUMPKIN

Pumpkin is a nutritious and healthy food option for dogs, and it can provide several health benefits.

Here are some benefits of feeding pumpkin to your dog:

1. Digestive health
Pumpkin is high in fiber, which can help regulate your dog's digestive system and prevent constipation and diarrhea. The soluble fiber content in pumpkin absorbs water, which can add bulk to your dog's stool and promote healthy bowel movements.

2. Vitamins and minerals
Pumpkin is a good source of vitamins A, C, and E, as well as minerals like iron and potassium, which can help support your dog's overall health and well-being.

3. Moisture
Pumpkin is high in moisture, which can help keep your dog hydrated and prevent urinary tract infections.

4. Skin and coat health
The nutrients in pumpkin, such as vitamin A and zinc, can help improve your dog's skin and coat health, making their fur shiny and healthy.

5. Weight management
Pumpkin is low in calories and can serve as a healthy, low-calorie snack for your dog, which can help with weight management.

However, it's important to note that pumpkin should be fed in moderation and prepared properly. Canned pumpkin is a great alternative if you do not have fresh pumpkin in stock. Additionally, pumpkin should not make up a significant portion of your dog's diet and should be given in moderation as a supplement to their regular dog food. Always consult with your veterinarian before introducing new foods to your dog's diet, especially if your dog has any specific dietary needs or health conditions.

Chicken and Zucchini Stir Fry with Fresh Rosemary

This recipe is nutritionally complete and balanced, and it yields approximately 4 cups of food, equating to 1,200 calories (Kcals), which is enough servings of food for one day for a 40 lb dog to maintain weight. It is also easy to make and a fan favorite, making it best for dogs with sensitive stomachs or those who are picky eaters.

Ingredients
- 1 pound boneless, skinless chicken breasts, cut into small pieces
- 2 cups zucchini, sliced
- 1 cup cooked brown rice
- 1 tablespoon olive oil
- 1 teaspoon dried basil

Optional Additions
- 1/4 cup cooked carrots, chopped
- 1/4 cup cooked green beans, chopped

Instructions
1. In a large skillet, heat the olive oil over medium heat.
2. Add the chicken pieces to the skillet and cook for 5-7 minutes, stirring occasionally, until browned and cooked through.
3. Add the sliced zucchini, brown rice, and dried basil to the skillet and stir to combine with the chicken.
4. If using, add the cooked carrots and green beans to the skillet and stir to combine.
5. Cook the mixture for an additional 2-3 minutes, until all the ingredients are well combined and heated through.
6. Remove the skillet from the heat and let the mixture cool before serving it to your dog.

Rosemary

Rosemary is generally considered safe for dogs in small amounts. Fresh or dried rosemary can be added to your dog's food as a flavor enhancer, and it may even have some health benefits. However, rosemary essential oil is not safe for dogs and should be avoided, whether ingested or applied topically. As with any dietary changes, it's best to consult your veterinarian before introducing rosemary or any other new ingredient to your dog's diet.

TURKEY
Turkey is generally considered good for dogs and can provide several health benefits. Here are some reasons why:

- Turkey is a good source of protein, riboflavin, and phosphorous, which can help support your dog's overall health and well-being.

- Turkey is a lean, healthy animal protein that is often a main ingredient in dog food recipes, and it can be given to your dog as a treat.

- Turkey is free from synthetic additives and preservatives, making it easier for your dog to digest and absorb the nutrients that lead to healing.

- When cooked and served correctly, turkey is not bad for dogs and can be a healthy, occasional treat for them.

However, it's important to note that how the turkey is cooked and seasoned can affect whether it is safe for dogs to eat.

For example, Thanksgiving turkeys are often seasoned with salt, pepper, herbs, and spices, which can be toxic to dogs and cause digestive upset or pancreatitis.

Additionally, turkey lunch meat and other processed turkey meat can contain high amounts of salt and preservatives that could be harmful to your dog's health.

As with any new food or ingredient, it's best to introduce turkey to your dog's diet slowly and in moderation, and to consult with your veterinarian if you have any concerns about your dog's health or dietary needs.

10

Turkey and Pea Stew with Rose Petals

Indulge your canine companion in the epitome of culinary excellence with my Turkey and Pea Stew with Rose Petals. Picture succulent pieces of perfectly cooked turkey, nestled amidst a medley of vibrant peas, all delicately infused with the fragrant essence of handpicked rose petals. This isn't just a meal; it's a symphony of flavors, a culinary masterpiece that transcends the ordinary. The tender turkey, the crisp sweetness of peas, and the subtle floral notes from the rose petals create a harmonious dance on your dog's palate. It's a feast that doesn't just satiate hunger; it elevates the dining experience for your four-legged friend. Treat them to this gastronomic delight, and watch as their tail wags in culinary approval.

Ingredients
- 1 pound ground turkey, cooked
- 2 cups peas, cooked
- 1 cup cooked brown rice
- 1 tablespoon olive oil
- 1 teaspoon dried thyme
- 1 solid pinch of Rose petals

Optional Additions
- 1/4 cup cooked carrots, chopped
- 1/4 cup cooked sweet potatoes, mashed or finely chopped

Instructions
1. In a large skillet, heat the olive oil over medium heat.
2. Add the cooked ground turkey to the skillet and cook for 5-7 minutes, stirring occasionally, until heated through.
3. Add the cooked peas, brown rice, and dried thyme to the skillet and stir to combine with the turkey.
4. If using, add the cooked carrots and sweet potatoes to the skillet and stir to combine.
5. Cook the mixture for an additional 2-3 minutes, until all the ingredients are well combined and heated through.
6. Remove the skillet from the heat and let the mixture cool before serving it to your dog.

Rose Petals

Rose petals are safe for dogs to eat and can make a colorful addition to their meals. However, make sure the roses are not treated with insecticides, fungicides, or weed-killers, as those can be harmful to your dog.

11

Beef and Carrot Stew with Snapdragons

Elevate your dog's dining experience with my Beef and Carrot Stew featuring a surprising touch of Snapdragons. This hearty stew boasts tender, slow-cooked beef, complemented by the natural sweetness of carrots, creating a symphony of flavors that'll have your furry friend begging for more. The addition of Snapdragons adds a unique twist, introducing a hint of floral notes to the dish. It's not just a stew; it's a culinary adventure for your dog's discerning palate. Treat them to this exceptional creation, and witness their delight with every savory bite.

The Snapdragons are sprinkled, fresh, over the prepared dish.

Ingredients
- 1 pound beef stew meat, cut into small pieces
- 2 cups carrots, sliced
- 1 cup cooked brown rice
- 1 tablespoon olive oil
- 1 teaspoon dried thyme
- 1 solid pinch of Snapdragons

Optional Additions
- 1/4 cup cooked green beans, chopped
- 1/4 cup cooked sweet potatoes, mashed or finely chopped

Instructions
1. In a large pot or Dutch oven, heat the olive oil over medium heat.
2. Add the beef stew meat to the pot and cook for 5-7 minutes, stirring occasionally, until browned on all sides.
3. Add the sliced carrots, brown rice, and dried thyme to the pot and stir to combine with the beef.
4. If using, add the cooked green beans and sweet potatoes to the pot and stir to combine.
5. Add enough water to the pot to cover the ingredients by about an inch.
6. Bring the mixture to a boil, then reduce the heat to low and let it simmer for 1-2 hours, or until the beef is tender and the vegetables are soft.
7. Remove the pot from the heat and let the stew cool before serving it to your dog.

Snapdragons

Snapdragons are considered a "self-seeding" annual flower and are safe for dogs to eat. They do best in full sun. However, make sure the snapdragons are not treated with insecticides, fungicides, or weed-killers, as those can be harmful to your dog.

12

Chicken and Sweet Potato Mash with Herbs

Indulge your canine companion with the exquisite flavors of my Chicken and Sweet Potato Mash with Herbs. Succulent, shredded chicken meets the velvety sweetness of mashed sweet potatoes, creating a delectable medley that your furry friend will find irresistible. Infused with a selection of aromatic herbs, this dish transforms mealtime into a culinary celebration for your four-legged family member. It's not just a meal; it's a symphony of flavors designed to satisfy and nourish. Treat your dog to this culinary delight, and watch their tail-wagging approval unfold with each delightful spoonful.

This recipe is nutritionally complete and balanced, and it yields approximately 4 cups of food, equating to 1,200 calories (Kcals), which is enough servings of food for one day for a 40 lb dog to maintain weight. It is also easy to make and a fan favorite, making it best for dogs with sensitive stomachs or those who are picky eaters.

Ingredients
- 1 pound boneless, skinless chicken breasts, cooked and shredded
- 2 cups sweet potatoes, cooked and mashed
- 1 tablespoon olive oil
- 1 teaspoon dried parsley
- 1 teaspoon dried basil

Optional Additions
- 1/4 cup cooked green beans, chopped
- 1/4 cup cooked carrots, chopped

Instructions
1. In a large skillet, heat the olive oil over medium heat.
2. Add the cooked and shredded chicken to the skillet and cook for 5-7 minutes, stirring occasionally, until heated through.
3. Add the mashed sweet potatoes, dried parsley, and dried basil to the skillet and stir to combine with the chicken.
4. If using, add the cooked green beans and carrots to the skillet and stir to combine.
5. Cook the mixture for an additional 2-3 minutes, until all the ingredients are well combined and heated through.
6. Remove the skillet from the heat and let the mixture cool before serving it to your dog.

This recipe is dog-safe because it uses fresh, whole food ingredients that are nutritionally balanced and free of any harmful additives or preservatives. It is also easy to digest and gentle on the stomach, making it ideal for dogs with sensitive digestive systems.

Variation
You can substitute the sweet potatoes with pumpkin or butternut squash for a different flavor.

Parsley

Parsley is generally considered good for dogs and can provide several health benefits. Here are some benefits of feeding parsley to your dog:

1. Anti-inflammatory and antimicrobial properties: Parsley has been found to have both anti-inflammatory and antimicrobial properties, making it a good substance for dogs who suffer from UTIs or arthritis to consume.

2. Rich in vitamins and minerals: Parsley is a nutritional powerhouse, containing large amounts of vitamin K, along with healthy amounts of vitamins C and A, and iron.

3. Freshens breath: Parsley is valued as a breath freshener and can help freshen your dog's breath.

4. Improves blood health: The high contents of chlorophyll in parsley make it excellent for improving the health of blood cells.

5. Relieves swelling and pain: Parsley can relieve swelling and pain from arthritis and other inflammatory conditions.

However, it's important to note that parsley should be fed in moderation and prepared properly. Only the curly variety of parsley should be fed to dogs, as the spring parsley can be toxic. Additionally, parsley should not make up a significant portion of your dog's diet and should be given in moderation as a supplement to their regular dog food. Always consult with your veterinarian before introducing new foods to your dog's diet, especially if your dog has any specific dietary needs or health conditions.

13

Turkey and Broccoli Stir Fry with Safe Spices

When it comes to crafting a delectable and nutritious Turkey and Broccoli Stir Fry for your canine companion, the key is to focus on safe ingredients and judicious use of spices. Turkey, a lean source of protein, serves as the star of this dish, providing essential nutrients for muscle health and overall well-being. Paired with nutrient-rich broccoli, this stir fry delivers a burst of vitamins and minerals.

Ingredients
- 1 pound ground turkey, cooked
- 2 cups broccoli florets, cooked and chopped
- 1 cup cooked brown rice
- 1 tablespoon olive oil
- 1 teaspoon dried oregano
- 1/2 teaspoon turmeric

Optional Additions
- 1/4 cup cooked carrots, chopped
- 1/4 cup cooked sweet potatoes, mashed or finely chopped

Instructions
1. In a large skillet, heat the olive oil over medium heat.
2. Add the cooked ground turkey to the skillet and cook for 5-7 minutes, stirring occasionally, until heated through.
3. Add the cooked broccoli florets, brown rice, dried oregano, and turmeric to the skillet and stir to combine with the turkey.
4. If using, add the cooked carrots and sweet potatoes to the skillet and stir to combine.
5. Cook the mixture for an additional 2-3 minutes, until all the ingredients are well combined and heated through.
6. Remove the skillet from the heat and let the mixture cool before serving it to your dog.

Broccoli

Broccoli is safe for dogs to eat, both cooked and raw, as long as it is given in small quantities and without any seasonings or oils. The vegetable is packed with vitamins and minerals, including fiber, vitamin C, and vitamin K, making it a healthy addition to your dog's diet.

However, the florets of broccoli contain isothiocyanates, which can cause mild-to-potentially-severe gastric irritation in some dogs, so it's important to feed them in moderation. Additionally, dogs should not rely on broccoli alone for their vitamins and minerals, and portion control is essential to avoid digestive issues.

14

Tripe and Chinese Vegetable Stew

Let me tell you, this dog-safe tripe recipe is an absolute game-changer for your four-legged friend. We're talking about a feast that's not only nutritionally complete and balanced but also bursting with flavor that will leave your pup's tail wagging in delight. Packed with protein, vitamins, and digestive goodness, this dish is a health powerhouse. And let's not forget the culinary finesse—it's easy to make, a fan favorite, perfect for those sensitive stomachs, and for the picky eaters, we've just unlocked their new obsession. This tripe sensation is a culinary triumph for your furry companion, delivering not just a meal but an unforgettable experience in each bowl.

Ingredients

- 1 pound tripe, cooked and chopped
- 2 cups Chinese vegetables (bok choy, napa cabbage, or baby bok choy), chopped
- 1 cup cooked brown rice
- 1 tablespoon olive oil
- 1 teaspoon dried ginger
- 1/2 teaspoon garlic powder

Optional Additions

- 1/4 cup cooked carrots, chopped
- 1/4 cup cooked sweet potatoes, mashed or finely chopped

Instructions

1. In a large pot or Dutch oven, heat the olive oil over medium heat.
2. Add the cooked and chopped tripe to the pot and cook for 5-7 minutes, stirring occasionally, until heated through.
3. Add the chopped Chinese vegetables, brown rice, dried ginger, and garlic powder to the pot and stir to combine with the tripe.
4. If using, add the cooked carrots and sweet potatoes to the pot and stir to combine.
5. Add enough water to the pot to cover the ingredients by about an inch.
6. Bring the mixture to a boil, then reduce the heat to low and let it simmer for 1-2 hours, or until the vegetables are soft.
7. Remove the pot from the heat and let the stew cool before serving it to your dog.

Chinese Vegetables

When preparing Chinese vegetables for your dog, opt for simple cooking methods like steaming or boiling without the addition of any seasonings or oils. These methods help retain the nutritional value of the vegetables while making them easily digestible for your furry friend. Always be mindful of portion sizes and introduce new vegetables gradually, observing your dog's response to ensure they tolerate the additions well.

Bok Choy: Bok choy is safe for dogs to eat in moderation and can provide various health benefits, such as being a good source of vitamins and minerals. It is best to feed dogs cooked bok choy and avoid adding any seasonings, garlic, or onions

Chinese Leaf: Chinese leaf, also known as Napa cabbage or Chinese cabbage, is another Chinese vegetable that is safe for dogs to eat. It is antioxidant-rich and high in vitamin C, making it a healthy addition to your dog's diet

When feeding your dog Chinese vegetables, it's important to prepare them without any seasonings, oils, garlic, or onions, as these can be harmful to dogs

Additionally, Chinese vegetables should not make up a significant portion of your dog's diet and should be given in moderation as a supplement to their regular dog food

Always consult with your veterinarian before introducing new foods to your dog's diet, especially if your dog has any specific dietary needs or health conditions.

Root Vegetables

Root vegetables are rich in essential nutrients, vitamins, and minerals that can contribute to a dog's overall health. They are also a good source of fiber and antioxidants, which can aid in digestion, boost the immune system, and help maintain the dog's health and wellbeing.

However, it's important to manage the amounts provided, as some root vegetables have high sugar content, and moderation is key to prevent any potential negative effects

Several root vegetables are safe for dogs and can be a nutritious addition to their diet. Here are some dog-safe root vegetables:

Carrots: Carrots are an excellent source of beta-carotene and are low in calories, making them a healthy and crunchy treat for dogs.

Sweet Potatoes: Rich in vitamins and fiber, sweet potatoes provide a tasty and nutritious option for dogs. They are often used in homemade dog food recipes.

Pumpkin: While technically a type of squash, pumpkin is a nutrient-rich root vegetable that is safe for dogs. It can be beneficial for digestive health.

Beets: Beets are a good source of vitamins and minerals. However, they are high in natural sugars, so moderation is key.

Turnips: Turnips are low in calories and provide vitamins and minerals. They can be cooked and added to your dog's meals.

Parsnips: Parsnips are another root vegetable that can be included in a dog's diet. They contain fiber and various nutrients.

Rutabaga: Rutabagas are a cross between turnips and cabbage, offering a mix of nutrients. They can be cooked and served to dogs in moderation.

15

Chicken and Root Vegetable Stew

This Chicken and Root Vegetable Stew is perfect for your best friend. It's packed with fat-free chicken, carrots, potatoes, and parsnips, providing a balanced and nutritious meal. The root vegetables add essential vitamins, minerals, and fiber, promoting good digestion and overall health for your dog. It's a paw-some dish that will have your dog licking the bowl clean!

Ingredients
- 1 pound boneless, skinless chicken breasts, cut into small pieces
- 2 cups root vegetables (carrots, sweet potatoes, turnips), chopped
- 1 cup cooked brown rice
- 1 tablespoon olive oil
- 1 teaspoon dried thyme

Optional Additions
- 1/4 cup cooked green beans, chopped
- 1/4 cup cooked peas

Instructions
1. In a large pot or Dutch oven, heat the olive oil over medium heat.
2. Add the chicken pieces to the pot and cook for 5-7 minutes, stirring occasionally, until browned on all sides.
3. Add the chopped root vegetables, brown rice, and dried thyme to the pot and stir to combine with the chicken.
4. If using, add the cooked green beans and peas to the pot and stir to combine.
5. Add enough water to the pot to cover the ingredients by about an inch.
6. Bring the mixture to a boil, then reduce the heat to low and let it simmer for 1-2 hours, or until the vegetables are soft.
7. Remove the pot from the heat and let the stew cool before serving it to your dog.

16

Turkey and Spinach Stew

This Turkey and Spinach Stew is a fantastic, nutritious option for your dog. Packed with ground turkey, brown rice, and an array of healthy vegetables including spinach, carrots, and peas, this recipe provides a well-balanced meal for your furry friend. The spinach and other vegetables offer essential vitamins and minerals, while the ground turkey serves as a high-quality protein source. It's a delicious and wholesome meal that your dog will love!

Ingredients
- 1 pound ground turkey
- 1 cup brown rice
- 3 cups low-sodium chicken broth
- 1 cup chopped sweet potatoes
- 1 cup chopped carrots
- 1 cup chopped green beans
- 1 cup chopped spinach

Instructions
1. In a large pot, cook the ground turkey over medium heat until browned. Make sure to crumble the turkey as it cooks.
2. Add the brown rice and chicken broth to the pot. Bring to a boil, then reduce heat to low and cover. Simmer for 20 minutes.
3. Add the sweet potatoes, carrots, and green beans to the pot. Cover and cook for an additional 20 minutes, or until the vegetables are tender.
4. Stir in the chopped spinach and cook for an additional 5 minutes, until the spinach is wilted.
5. Allow the stew to cool before serving it to your dog. Store any leftovers in an airtight container in the refrigerator for up to 3 days, or in the freezer for up to 3 months.

Spinach

Spinach is generally considered safe for dogs to eat in moderation. Spinach is a leafy green vegetable that is high in vitamins A, B, C, and K, iron, antioxidants, beta-carotene, and roughage, which stimulate the digestive tract.

Spinach is a nutrient-dense food that can provide many health benefits to dogs, such as improving their digestive system, fighting obesity, and supporting their overall health and well-being.

However, spinach should only be fed to dogs in small portions, as it is high in oxalates, which can affect their metabolism and cause kidney damage and failure if consumed in large amounts.

17

Beef and Green Bean Stew

This recipe is nutritionally complete and balanced, and it yields approximately 4 cups of food, equating to 1,200 calories (Kcals), which is enough servings of food for one day for a 40 lb dog to maintain weight. It is also easy to make and a fan favorite, making it best for dogs with sensitive stomachs or those who are picky eaters.

Ingredients
- 1 pound beef stew meat, cut into small pieces
- 2 cups green beans, chopped
- 1 cup cooked brown rice
- 1 tablespoon olive oil
- 1 teaspoon dried rosemary

Optional Additions:
- 1/4 cup cooked carrots, chopped
- 1/4 cup cooked sweet potatoes, mashed or finely chopped

Instructions
1. In a large pot or Dutch oven, heat the olive oil over medium heat.
2. Add the beef stew meat to the pot and cook for 5-7 minutes, stirring occasionally, until browned on all sides.
3. Add the chopped green beans, brown rice, and dried rosemary to the pot and stir to combine with the beef.
4. If using, add the cooked carrots and sweet potatoes to the pot and stir to combine.
5. Add enough water to the pot to cover the ingredients by about an inch.
6. Bring the mixture to a boil, then reduce the heat to low and let it simmer for 1-2 hours, or until the beef is tender and the vegetables are soft.
7. Remove the pot from the heat and let the stew cool before serving it to your dog.

Green Beans

Raw green beans are actually a little bit toxic. They contain a small amount of poison, which is more concentrated in the seeds than in the pod. However, cooking green beans breaks down the toxins, making them safe to eat. So, while you won't die from eating raw green beans, it's best to enjoy them cooked to fully savor their delicious flavor and nutritional benefits

Cooked green beans are good for dogs.

They are a healthy, low-calorie vegetable that is safe for dogs to eat. Green beans are packed with essential vitamins and minerals, including protein, iron, calcium, and vitamins B6, A, C, and K. They are also a good source of minerals, such as manganese, which supports metabolism and has antioxidant abilities, as well as bone health and wound healing.

Green beans can be fed to dogs in various forms, including raw, cooked, canned, steamed, blanched, or pureed. However, it is important to feed them plain and avoid adding any harmful ingredients, such as salt, oils, spices, garlic, or onions. Canned green beans, in particular, should be avoided due to their high salt content.

When introducing green beans to your dog's diet, start with small amounts and monitor their reaction. Some dogs may not enjoy the taste of green beans, while others may love them as a healthy treat. As with all foods, moderation is key, and green beans should be fed as part of a balanced diet, with 75-85% of a dog's diet being meat-based. If you have any concerns or questions about feeding green beans to your dog, consult your veterinarian for personalized advice.

18
Chicken and Three Vegetables

There are easy recipes and there are more complex recipes in this book. This one is easy. Classic. Always well received.

This recipe is dog-safe because it uses fresh, whole food ingredients that are nutritionally balanced and free of any harmful additives or preservatives. It is also easy to digest and gentle on the stomach, making it ideal for dogs with sensitive digestive systems.

Ingredients
- 1 pound boneless, skinless chicken breasts, cut into small pieces
- 1 cup cooked brown rice
- 3 cups low-sodium chicken broth
- 1 cup chopped sweet potatoes
- 1 cup chopped carrots
- 1 cup chopped green beans

Instructions
1. In a large pot, cook the chicken over medium heat until browned. Make sure to crumble the chicken as it cooks[1].
2. Add the brown rice and chicken broth to the pot. Bring to a boil, then reduce heat to low and cover. Simmer for 20 minutes.
3. Add the sweet potatoes, carrots, and green beans to the pot. Cover and cook for an additional 20 minutes, or until the vegetables are tender.
4. Allow the stew to cool before serving it to your dog. Store any leftovers in an airtight container in the refrigerator for up to 3 days, or in the freezer for up to 3 months[6].

Variation
You can substitute the chicken with other dog-safe proteins, such as turkey or beef. You can also add other dog-safe vegetables, such as peas or zucchini, to this stew. Just make sure to chop them into small, bite-sized pieces for easy digestion by your dog.

To freeze the stew, let it cool completely and then transfer it to an airtight container or freezer-safe zip-top bag. Label the container or bag with the date and contents, and store it in the freezer for up to three months. To thaw the stew, place it in the refrigerator overnight. Once thawed, you can reheat it on the stove before serving it to your dog. The stew can be stored in the refrigerator for up to three days.

Brown Rice

Brown rice is a healthy addition to most dogs' diets. It is an easily digestible carbohydrate that provides beneficial minerals, B vitamins, and fiber. Brown rice is also a good source of energy and can help overweight pets feel full and shed extra pounds. However, if your dog has an upset stomach, it's recommended to use white rice instead, as it contains less fiber and is gentler on the digestive system..

Benefits

1. Fiber for Digestive Health: Brown rice is a good source of fiber, which is beneficial for maintaining healthy digestion in dogs. The fiber content helps regulate bowel movements and can alleviate constipation, contributing to overall gastrointestinal health.

2. Essential Nutrients: Brown rice provides essential amino acids, B vitamins (such as niacin and thiamine), magnesium, and manganese, which are important for various bodily functions in dogs. These nutrients support energy production, a healthy coat, and overall well-being.

3. Sustained Energy: As a low-calorie, easily digestible carbohydrate, brown rice serves as a sustained energy source for dogs. It can help maintain their energy levels without causing rapid spikes and drops in blood sugar, keeping them active and alert.

4. Weight Management: For overweight dogs, brown rice can be a beneficial addition to their diet. It provides a feeling of fullness without excess calories, supporting weight management and helping dogs feel satisfied with their meals.

5. Cholesterol Regulation: Brown rice may help in regulating cholesterol levels in dogs, contributing to heart health. The fiber and beneficial nutrients in brown rice can aid in managing cholesterol, promoting cardiovascular well-being.

These benefits highlight the nutritional value of brown rice for dogs, making it a wholesome and supportive component of their diet when incorporated in appropriate proportions.

19
Pulled Turkey and Tofu

This Pulled Turkey and Tofu recipe is the mash-up what your Age of Aquarius-minded Fido has been looking for. It's a protein-packed delight featuring boneless, skinless turkey breasts and firm tofu, providing a balanced and nutritious meal. The addition of low-sodium chicken broth, carrots, and green beans ensures a burst of flavor and essential nutrients. This recipe is a testament to the fact that our dogs deserve the best, and this dish delivers just that. It's a culinary masterpiece that will have your dogs licking their bowls clean and wagging their tails for more!

Ingredients
- 1 pound boneless, skinless turkey breasts
- 1 block of firm tofu, drained and pressed
- 2 cups low-sodium chicken broth
- 1 cup chopped carrots
- 1 cup chopped green beans
- 1 tablespoon olive oil
- 1 teaspoon dried thyme

Instructions
1. Preheat the oven to 350°F.
2. Place the turkey breasts in a baking dish and pour the chicken broth over them.
3. Cover the dish with foil and bake for 1-2 hours, or until the turkey is cooked through and tender.
4. Remove the turkey from the dish and let it cool. Once it's cool enough to handle, shred the turkey into small pieces.
5. In a large skillet, heat the olive oil over medium heat.
6. Add the chopped carrots and green beans to the skillet and cook for 5-7 minutes, or until the vegetables are tender.
7. Add the shredded turkey and crumbled tofu to the skillet and stir to combine with the vegetables.
8. Add the dried thyme to the skillet and stir to combine.
9. Cook the mixture for an additional 2-3 minutes, until all the ingredients are well combined and heated through.
10. Remove the skillet from the heat and let the mixture cool before serving it to your dog.

Tofu, also known as bean curd, is made from soy milk pressed together to form a solid block. It is a popular plant-based protein worldwide, specifically in Asian countries. Tofu is a complete vegan protein made from soybeans and can take on the flavor of different ingredients, making it an ideal addition to a variety of dishes for people. Tofu's spongy and soft texture may not appeal to everyone, and it can take time to acquire a taste for it. Similarly, some dogs may not enjoy the texture of tofu, especially if it is mushy or uncooked. When introducing tofu to your dog, it's important to start with small quantities and observe their response to it. As with any new food, individual preferences and tolerances can vary, so it's best to monitor your dog's reaction to tofu to determine if it suits their palate and digestion.

Tofu

Opt for firm or extra firm tofu varieties as they are easier to handle and can be cut into smaller, bite-sized pieces for your dog.

According to current research, tofu is safe for dogs to eat in moderation. It is not toxic to them, but it does not contain enough protein to fulfill their nutritional requirements. While it is safe for dogs to eat tofu occasionally, it should not be the main protein in their diet.

It is important to note that soy is not a complete protein for dogs, so if your dog eats tofu, they may experience a mild case of gas or a more severe case of bloat. Therefore, it is recommended to feed tofu to dogs in moderation and as part of a balanced diet that includes other sources of protein.

In summary, tofu is safe for dogs to eat in moderation, but it should not be the main protein in their diet. It is important to ensure that your dog's diet is nutritionally complete and balanced, and to consult with a veterinarian before making any significant changes to their diet.

20

Beef, Pea, and Dog-Safe Dumpling Stew

A few obvious notes, here: Plain dumplings without any harmful ingredients may be safe for dogs to eat, but dumplings that contain onions, garlic, or other harmful ingredients should be avoided. That being said, plain dumplings that soak up flavor are fun foods for dogs of all sizes and breeds.

Ingredients
- 1 pound beef stew meat, cut into small pieces
- 2 cups frozen peas
- 1 cup chopped carrots
- 1 cup chopped sweet potatoes
- 1 tablespoon olive oil
- 1 teaspoon dried thyme
- 1 cup all-purpose flour
- 1/2 teaspoon baking powder
- 1/2 teaspoon salt
- 1/2 cup water

Instructions
1. In a large pot or Dutch oven, heat the olive oil over medium heat.
2. Add the beef stew meat to the pot and cook for 5-7 minutes, stirring occasionally, until browned on all sides.
3. Add the chopped carrots, sweet potatoes, and dried thyme to the pot and stir to combine with the beef.
4. Add enough water to the pot to cover the ingredients by about an inch.
5. Bring the mixture to a boil, then reduce the heat to low and let it simmer for 1-2 hours, or until the beef is tender and the vegetables are soft.
6. Add the frozen peas to the pot and stir to combine.
7. In a separate bowl, whisk together the flour, baking powder, and salt.
8. Add the water to the bowl and stir until a dough forms.
9. Drop spoonfuls of the dough onto the surface of the stew.
10. Cover the pot and let the dumplings cook for 10-15 minutes, or until they are cooked through.

21

Chicken and Garden Vegetable Stir Fry

Ah, brace yourself for the exquisite symphony of flavors in this Chicken and Garden Vegetable Stir Fry! A culinary masterpiece that harmoniously combines succulent chicken with a vibrant array of fresh garden vegetables. Each crisp, colorful bite is a celebration of textures and tastes, and the aromatic dance of spices elevates this dish to a culinary crescendo. It's not just a meal; it's a sensory journey that will have your dog's tail wagging in delight!

Ingredients
- 1 pound boneless, skinless chicken breasts, cut into small pieces
- 2 cups chopped mixed vegetables (such as carrots, green beans, and zucchini)
- 1 cup cooked brown rice
- 1 tablespoon olive oil
- 1 teaspoon dried thyme

Instructions
1. In a large skillet, heat the olive oil over medium heat.
2. Add the chicken to the skillet and cook for 5-7 minutes, stirring occasionally, until browned on all sides.
3. Add the chopped mixed vegetables to the skillet and stir to combine with the chicken.
4. Add the dried thyme to the skillet and stir to combine.
5. Cook the mixture for an additional 5-7 minutes, until the vegetables are tender and the chicken is cooked through.
6. Add the cooked brown rice to the skillet and stir to combine with the chicken and vegetables.
7. Remove the skillet from the heat and let the mixture cool before serving it to your dog.

THYME

Thyme is generally considered safe for dogs in small amounts, according to most sources.

Thyme has many health benefits for dogs, including its antifungal, antimicrobial, and antioxidant effects. Thyme contains antioxidants and certain compounds that might have anti-inflammatory properties. Thyme can create a more healthy digestive tract, help with irritable bowels, and aid in ousting parasites such as hookworm.

However, it is important to use thyme in moderation and never give it in excess. Thyme should be served in small amounts, such as ½ to 1 teaspoon every few days. Thyme contains vitamin K, iron, manganese, calcium, and dietary fiber, and thymol, the herb's primary active ingredient, helps inhibit the growth of fungus and bacteria.

While thyme is generally considered safe for dogs, it is important to avoid giving your dog thyme if they have a history of allergies or if they are pregnant or nursing. If you have any concerns or questions about feeding thyme to your dog, consult your veterinarian for personalized advice.

Cauliflower Mash with Mixed-Meat Porridge

Cauliflower in a mixed meat bowl for dogs isn't just a culinary choice; it's a canine delight! Dogs may love cauliflower for several reasons. First and foremost, its mild flavor complements the savory goodness of mixed meats, creating a palatable medley that satisfies their taste buds. Moreover, cauliflower adds a delightful crunch, introducing a textural contrast that keeps mealtime interesting. Beyond its taste and texture, cauliflower is a nutritional powerhouse, boasting vitamins, minerals, and fiber, contributing to a well-rounded and balanced canine diet. So, it's not just about love; it's a smart choice for a tasty and nutritious canine dining experience!

Ingredients
- 1 head of cauliflower, cut into florets
- 1 cup of mixed meat (such as chicken, beef, or turkey), cooked and shredded
- 1 cup of mixed vegetables (such as peas, carrots, and green beans), cooked and mashed
- 1/4 cup of low-sodium chicken or beef broth
- 1 tablespoon of olive oil

Instructions
1. Steam the cauliflower florets until they are tender. Drain and transfer them to a large bowl.

2. Use a potato masher or a food processor to mash the cauliflower until it reaches a smooth consistency. Set aside.

3. In a separate bowl, mix the cooked and shredded mixed meat with the mashed mixed vegetables.

4. Heat the low-sodium chicken or beef broth in a saucepan over medium heat. Add the mixed meat and vegetable mixture to the saucepan and cook for 5-7 minutes, or until heated through.

5. In a large skillet, heat the olive oil over medium heat. Add the mashed cauliflower to the skillet and cook for 3-5 minutes, or until heated through.

6. Serve the cauliflower mash with the mixed meat porridge on top. Allow the mixture to cool before serving it to your dog.

Turkey and Cauliflower Mash with Blueberries

23

IMPORTANT NOTICE:

Berries that are safe for dogs: include Blueberries, Blackberries, Strawberries and Raspberries. Berries that are not safe for dogs include Grapes and Raisins, Cherries and Wild Berries.

Ingredients
- 1 pound ground turkey
- 1 small head of cauliflower, cut into florets
- 1 cup blueberries (fresh or frozen)
- 1 tablespoon olive oil

Instructions:
1. In a large skillet, heat the olive oil over medium heat. Add the ground turkey and cook until browned and cooked through. Remove from the skillet and set aside.

2. In the same skillet, add the cauliflower florets and cook until tender, about 8-10 minutes. Remove from the heat and let cool slightly.

3. In a blender or food processor, combine the cooked cauliflower and blueberries. Blend until smooth and creamy.

4. In a large bowl, mix the ground turkey and cauliflower-blueberry mixture until well combined.

5. Serve the Turkey and Cauliflower Mash with Blueberries to your dog, either as a standalone meal or as a topper for their regular kibble.

Blueberries

Blueberries can be a delightful and nutritious addition to your dog's diet. Packed with antioxidants, vitamins C and K, and fiber, these little blue gems offer a boost to your dog's immune system and overall health. The natural sweetness of blueberries makes them a tasty treat that many dogs enjoy. Additionally, blueberries contain flavonoids that may contribute to cognitive function, which can be especially beneficial for senior dogs. Remember, moderation is key, and always consult with your veterinarian to ensure that blueberries align with your dog's dietary needs and any specific health considerations.

Carrot and Thyme Terrine with Blueberry

Now, here's a creation that will make your dog's taste buds stand to attention. We're breaking culinary boundaries for your furry friend with this sophisticated yet dog-safe recipe. Carrots bring a punch of vitamins and fiber, while blueberries add a burst of antioxidants. Oats contribute protein and fiber, and thyme steps in as a natural anti-inflammatory, perfect for aiding digestion.

Ingredients:
- 2 cups grated carrots
- 1/2 cup fresh blueberries
- 1/2 cup rolled oats
- 1/4 cup fresh thyme leaves
- 2 eggs

Instructions:
1. Preheat the oven to 350°F (175°C).
2. In a bowl, combine grated carrots, blueberries, rolled oats, and thyme leaves.
3. In a separate bowl, beat the eggs and add them to the carrot mixture. Mix thoroughly.
4. Pour the mixture into a greased loaf pan, smoothing the top.
5. Bake for 30-35 minutes until the terrine is firm and golden brown.
6. Let it cool completely before slicing and serving to your dog.

Freezing and Thawing:
Slice the terrine, wrap each portion tightly in plastic wrap, and freeze in a container for up to 3 months. Thaw slices in the refrigerator overnight.

Storage:
The terrine stays fresh for up to 5 days in the refrigerator and up to 3 months in the freezer. Now, that's haute cuisine for your canine companion.

Rolled Oats

Rolled oats can be a healthy addition to a dog's diet when fed in moderation. Oats are a good source of fiber, which can aid in digestion and help maintain a healthy digestive system for dogs. Additionally, oats provide some essential nutrients such as vitamins, minerals, and antioxidants.

When incorporating rolled oats into your dog's meals, it's important to cook or soak them to enhance digestibility. Raw oats may be difficult for dogs to digest and can potentially lead to gastrointestinal upset. Cooking or soaking the oats makes them softer and more palatable for your dog.

Brown Rice Bake with Game Meats and Raspberry

25

Ladies and gentlemen, gather 'round for a culinary masterpiece designed exclusively for your four-legged companions – the Brown Rice Bake with Game Meats and Raspberry. Picture this: wholesome brown rice, succulent game meats, and the sweet kiss of raspberries, all meticulously crafted to create a symphony of flavors and nutrition. This dish isn't just a meal; it's a gastronomic journey for your beloved pets. The brown rice provides a hearty base, while game meats offer a protein-packed punch, and raspberries add a touch of sweetness and antioxidants. It's a culinary delight that transcends the ordinary, tailored for discerning canine palates. Serve up a feast fit for royalty and watch tails wag with delight – because when it comes to exceptional dog cuisine, this Brown Rice Bake takes the crown!

Ingredients
- 2 cups cooked brown rice
- 1/2 cup cooked game meats (such as venison or bison)
- 1/2 cup fresh raspberries
- 1/4 cup chopped parsley
- 2 eggs

Instructions
1. Preheat the oven to 350°F (175°C).
2. In a large bowl, mix together the cooked brown rice, game meats, raspberries, and chopped parsley.
3. Beat the eggs in a separate bowl and add them to the rice mixture. Mix well.
4. Pour the mixture into a greased baking dish and smooth the top.
5. Bake for 30-35 minutes, or until the bake is firm and golden brown.
6. Let the bake cool completely before serving to your dog.

Raspberries

Raspberries are generally considered safe for dogs to eat in moderation. Raspberries are a good source of antioxidants, fiber, manganese, and vitamin C, which can help improve your dog's digestive system, fight obesity, and support their overall health and well-being.

However, raspberries are also high in sugar, so they should be given as a treat and not as a regular part of your dog's diet. It's important to wash the raspberries thoroughly and remove any stems or leaves before feeding them to your dog.

26

Roasted Game Bird with Dog-Safe Herbs and Spices

Get ready to elevate your canine's dining experience with the Roasted Game Bird with Dog-Safe Herbs and Spices – a culinary sensation designed exclusively for our four-legged friends. This recipe is meticulously crafted, ensuring every ingredient is not just delectable but safe for your precious pooch. The game bird takes center stage, delivering a protein-packed punch, while a medley of dog-safe herbs, including parsley, thyme, or rosemary, adds a symphony of flavors. But here's the magic touch – a dash of turmeric or ginger, natural anti-inflammatories that champion digestive health and joint well-being. It's a culinary masterpiece that promises not just a meal but a canine celebration. Prepare to witness tail-wagging ecstasy as your furry companion indulges in the extraordinary – because, in the world of dog cuisine, this Roasted Game Bird reigns supreme.

When feeding your dog an occasional game bird, several benefits can be observed. Game birds offer a different nutritional profile compared to traditional meats, providing a diverse range of essential nutrients that can contribute to your dog's overall health. They are typically leaner than domesticated meats, making them an excellent source of high-quality protein for your dog's muscle development and maintenance. Additionally, game birds are a natural prey for dogs, and consuming them can mimic their ancestral diet, providing a more natural and species-appropriate food option. However, it's important to ensure that the meat is fresh, properly handled, and free from any harmful parasites or diseases. Always consult with your veterinarian before making significant changes to your dog's diet to ensure it aligns with their specific nutritional needs and overall well-being.

Ingredients
- 1 game bird (such as quail or pheasant)
- 1/4 cup chopped dog-safe herbs (such as parsley, thyme, or rosemary)
- 1/4 tsp dog-safe spice (such as turmeric or ginger)

Instructions
1. Preheat the oven to 375°F (190°C).
2. Rinse the game bird and pat it dry with paper towels.
3. Rub the chopped herbs and spice all over the bird, making sure to get it into the crevices and under the skin.
4. Place the bird on a roasting pan and roast for 25-30 minutes, or until the internal temperature reaches 165°F (74°C).
5. Let the bird cool for a few minutes before serving to your dog.

10 SPICES
THAT ARE UNSAFE FOR DOGS

The following herbs and spices are unsafe for dogs:

1. Nutmeg: Can cause a severe upset stomach for dogs and extensive damage to the nervous system.

2. Salt: In large quantities, salt can be harmful to dogs.

3. Cocoa Powder: Contains theobromine, which is toxic to dogs and can cause various symptoms, including vomiting, diarrhea, and even seizures.

4. Paprika: While not toxic, it can cause stomach upset in dogs.

5. Oregano: When used improperly, oregano can be toxic to dogs and cause gastrointestinal issues such as vomiting and diarrhea.

6. Tea tree oil: 100% tea tree oil is extremely toxic to dogs and can cause tremors, ataxia, and coma.

7. Hops: Hops are toxic to dogs and can cause an elevated temperature, seizures, or death.

8. Chamomile: Chamomile is toxic to dogs and can cause vomiting, diarrhea, and skin irritation.

9. Chives: Chives, along with other allium family members, can be toxic to dogs, leading to symptoms such as gastrointestinal upset, red blood cell damage, and even organ damage.

10. Onion and Garlic: Onions and garlic are avoided for dogs due to their potential toxicity. Both onions and garlic contain compounds that can cause damage to a dog's red blood cells, leading to a condition called hemolytic anemia. This can result in symptoms such as weakness, lethargy, and pale gums, and in severe cases, it can be life-threatening. Therefore, it's important to keep these ingredients away from dogs to ensure their safety and well-being. Always consult with a veterinarian if you suspect your dog has ingested onions or garlic or if you have any concerns about their diet.

This is to be considered a partial list. It is important to consult with your veterinarian before adding any herbs to your dog's diet. Even safe herbs should be used in moderation and with caution, as some dogs may have allergies or sensitivities to certain herbs. When using herbs, always follow the recommended dosage and preparation instructions to avoid any potential health risks.

Beef and Barley and Carrot

27

Indulge your canine companion in a culinary experience that blends the richness of hearty beef, the wholesome goodness of barley, and the vibrant crunch of sweet carrots. This nutritionally balanced meal is not just a treat for the taste buds but a symphony of essential nutrients for your dog's well-being. The tender beef provides high-quality protein, while barley delivers a punch of energy and digestive support. Carrots add a delightful burst of flavor and a dose of vitamins, making this a complete and satisfying feast that your dog will eagerly wag their tail for. Elevate their dining experience with the finest ingredients crafted into a delicious harmony – because your furry friend deserves nothing but the best.

Ingredients
- 1 pound ground beef
- 1 cup cooked barley
- 1 cup chopped carrots
- 1/4 cup chopped dog-safe herbs (such as parsley or thyme)
- 1/4 tsp dog-safe spice (such as turmeric or ginger)

Instructions
1. Preheat the oven to 375°F (190°C).
2. In a large skillet, cook the ground beef over medium heat until browned.
3. Add the cooked barley, chopped carrots, chopped herbs, and spice to the skillet. Mix well.
4. Transfer the mixture to a greased baking dish and smooth the top.
5. Bake for 25-30 minutes, or until the bake is firm and golden brown.
6. Let the bake cool completely before serving to your dog.

Barley

Barley, my dear, is a fantastic addition to your dog's diet—here's why. Packed with dietary fiber, B vitamins, and essential minerals, it's a nutritional powerhouse that brings more to the table than just a delightful chew. Unlike some starchy counterparts, barley offers excellent digestibility and scores low on the glycemic index—a win for maintaining steady blood sugar levels.

Now, let's talk about that soluble fiber; it's the hero supporting your dog's digestive health, ensuring things run smoothly. But the goodness doesn't stop there—antioxidants, iron, and manganese make their grand entrance, contributing to your dog's overall well-being.

However, and pay close attention, moderation is key. Barley should play a supporting role, not steal the show. While serving, ensure it's rinsed and cooked, keeping it free from ingredients like garlic, onion, or overly zealous spices. And when opting for store-bought goodies, check the label—meat should lead the cast.

In the culinary world, balance is everything, and the same applies to your dog's diet. Barley, in moderation, adds a touch of wholesome goodness, turning an ordinary meal into a feast fit for a discerning pooch.

28

Chicken, Quinoa and Kale

Right, let's dive into this Chicken and Quinoa Extravaganza! First off, we've got boneless, skinless chicken breasts—now, crucial here is to give those chicken pieces a golden brown sear, infusing that skillet with flavor, bringing out the succulence in every bite. Next up, the quinoa! A fabulous addition, providing a wholesome dose of protein and a delightful texture that'll make your dog's taste buds dance.

But hold on, we're not done. Carrots, my dear, add a splash of color and a burst of natural sweetness. We're not just cooking here; we're crafting a palette of tastes and textures. Now, pay attention to those dog-safe herbs—no bland meals here! A sprinkle of parsley or thyme elevates this dish to gourmet levels.

And the spice, ah, the secret weapon! Turmeric or ginger, both not only lend a distinct flavor but also boast anti-inflammatory properties. We're not just serving food; we're serving wellness.

Cooking time, it's a bit of patience, but trust me, every second is worth it. You want those carrots tender, the chicken cooked to perfection. And don't you dare forget the cooling stage—it's the moment when flavors settle and intertwine, creating a symphony of canine delight.

In essence, this isn't just a recipe; it's a culinary masterpiece for your four-legged friend. An ensemble of quality ingredients, a touch of finesse, and a dash of love—because every dog deserves a gourmet experience at mealtime.

Ingredients
- 1 pound boneless, skinless chicken breasts, cut into small pieces
- 1 cup cooked quinoa
- 1 cup chopped carrots
- 1/4 cup chopped dog-safe herbs (such as parsley or thyme)
- 1/4 tsp dog-safe spice (such as turmeric or ginger)

Instructions
1. In a large skillet, cook the chicken over medium heat until browned.
2. Add the cooked quinoa, chopped carrots, chopped herbs, and spice to the skillet. Mix well.
3. Cook for an additional 10-15 minutes, or until the carrots are tender and the chicken is cooked through.
4. Let the mixture cool completely before serving to your dog.

29 Banana and Chicken

Bananarama! Now, this banana and chicken concoction might just be the canine treat of the century, but let's break it down with a bit of culinary finesse.

Bananas, a delightful fruit, bring more than just sweetness to the table. They're packed with potassium, vitamins B6 and C, fiber, and magnesium—an ensemble that can certainly bolster your dog's overall health. However, here's the rub: bananas, though full of goodness, come with a sugar kick. So, consider them a special treat, not the star of the show.

Now, for the chicken, my absolute favorite protein. Baked to perfection, it adds that savory touch that dogs simply can't resist. Shred it into a luscious consistency, blend it with the smooth, ripe banana, and voilà—a treat that's not just tasty but a nutritional powerhouse.

A word of advice: as with any culinary masterpiece, moderation is key. Peel those bananas, cut them into dog-friendly sizes, and introduce this divine duo slowly. And, of course, consult your veterinarian if you have any concerns.

Banana and chicken, my friends—a treat that's music to your dog's taste buds and a symphony of health benefits in every bite.

Ingredients
- 1 boneless, skinless chicken breast
- 1 ripe banana

Instructions
1. Preheat your oven to 350°F (175°C).
2. Place the chicken breast on a baking sheet and bake for 20-25 minutes, or until cooked through. Let it cool.
3. In a blender or food processor, blend the cooked chicken until it reaches a shredded consistency.
4. Mash the ripe banana with a fork until smooth.
5. In a mixing bowl, combine the shredded chicken and mashed banana. Mix well until the ingredients are evenly distributed.
6. Scoop the mixture into silicone molds or ice cube trays for portion control.
7. Place the molds or trays in the freezer and let them freeze for at least 2 hours, or until solid.
8. Once frozen, remove the treats from the molds or trays and store them in an airtight container or freezer bag in the freezer.

Why is this a dog-safe recipe?
- Chicken is a lean source of protein that is safe for dogs to consume in moderation.
- Bananas are a good source of vitamins and minerals, such as potassium and vitamin C, which can benefit dogs in small amounts.

Coconut

Coconut, my friends, a tropical gem that can tantalize taste buds and bring a myriad of health benefits to our canine companions. Let's dissect this coconut magic with a dash of culinary wisdom.

First and foremost, healthy fats! Yes, you heard it right. Coconut is a treasure trove of good fats, alongside a symphony of vitamins and minerals—a concoction that can certainly elevate your dog's overall well-being.

Now, let's talk about medium-chain triglycerides (MCTs)—the secret sauce in coconut. These bad boys can fuel your dog's energy levels and even sharpen their cognitive function. Think of it as a brain-boosting piña colada for your furry friend.

But wait, there's more! Anti-inflammatory properties—coconut is a natural soother, perfect for those dogs with cuts, wounds, or hot spots. It's like a tropical spa day for your pooch's skin.

And here's the grand finale—joint pain relief. Coconut swoops in as a hero for dogs grappling with arthritis or other inflammatory conditions, offering comfort and support.

But, my friends, a word of caution. As with any culinary adventure, moderation is the golden rule. Introduce coconut slowly, savor the benefits, and, of course, consult your trusted veterinarian if you have any concerns about your dog's health or dietary needs.

Coconut, a tropical delight that's not just a flavor bomb but a wellness elixir for your beloved four-legged companion.

30 Coconut Chicken

Ah, coconut chicken, a dish that marries the indulgence of coconut with the savory allure of chicken. Now, let me sprinkle some culinary insight into this delectable concoction.

Coconut oil, my dear friends, is the star of the show. A powerhouse of energy and a true champion for your dog's skin and coat. Picture this: a delectable blend of fatty acids and healthy saturated fats working in harmony to banish allergies and soothe that pesky itch. It's like a spa day for your canine companion.

But that's not all—coconut oil takes on the role of a digestive maestro, boosting immunity, energizing your pup, and even sending fleas and ticks packing. Now, that's what I call a versatile kitchen companion!

However, a word of caution. Just like in the culinary world, too much of a good thing can upset the balance. Introduce coconut oil gradually, savor the benefits, and always consult your trusted veterinarian before embarking on this culinary adventure.

Now, onto our masterpiece—coconut chicken. A symphony of flavors where succulent chicken meets the tropical embrace of coconut. These treats, my friends, are not just a feast for the taste buds but a celebration of well-being for your four-legged friend.

Picture this—shredded chicken, coconut flakes, coconut flour, and the magic touch of melted coconut oil, all dancing together in harmony. The result? Golden-brown, firm treats that are a testament to the marriage of health and flavor.

Serve them to your dog, and watch as tails wag in approval. Coconut chicken, a culinary masterpiece for your discerning canine connoisseur.

Ingredients
- 1 cup cooked chicken, shredded or diced
- 1/4 cup unsweetened coconut flakes
- 1/4 cup coconut flour
- 1/4 cup coconut oil, melted
- 1/4 cup chicken broth, low sodium
- 1/4 cup water

Instructions
1. Preheat your oven to 350°F (175°C) and line a baking sheet with parchment paper.
2. In a large bowl, combine the cooked chicken, coconut flakes, coconut flour, melted coconut oil, chicken broth, and water. Mix well until all the ingredients are evenly incorporated.
3. Scoop out tablespoon-sized portions of the mixture and place them on the prepared baking sheet. Flatten each portion with the back of a spoon to form a small, round cookie shape.
4. Bake the treats in the preheated oven for 15-20 minutes, or until they are golden brown and firm to the touch.
5. Remove the treats from the oven and let them cool completely before serving to your dog.

Mixed Meats with Coconut and Peas

Now, let's talk about a true canine delight—mixed meat and pea treats. A symphony of flavors that will have your dog's taste buds doing a standing ovation. Pay attention, because this one's a culinary masterpiece.

Imagine a blend of succulent mixed meats—chicken, beef, or turkey—skillfully shredded or diced to perfection. Then, in comes the peas, adding a burst of freshness and a touch of vibrancy to our culinary canvas. But we're not stopping there; here comes the coconut trio—flakes, flour, and oil, working together like a culinary dream team.

Now, let's talk coconut oil. Melted to perfection, it not only adds richness but also brings a host of health benefits. From improving skin and coat to energizing your pup, it's a true game-changer.

And the binding element? A touch of low-sodium chicken broth or, for the true connoisseur, your very own chicken bone broth. We're not settling for mediocrity here; we're crafting treats that are both exquisite in flavor and packed with goodness.

Form these morsels into delightful, round shapes, bake until golden brown, and voilà—canine-friendly treats that are nothing short of a gourmet experience. Your dog deserves nothing but the best, and these treats are a testament to that philosophy.

So, my friends, present these treats to your furry companions, and watch as they indulge in a culinary journey designed for their discerning palates. Mixed meat and pea treats—a true feast for your four-legged connoisseur.

Ingredients
- 1 cup cooked mixed meats (such as chicken, beef, or turkey), shredded or diced
- 1/2 cup cooked peas
- 1/4 cup unsweetened coconut flakes
- 1/4 cup coconut flour
- 1/4 cup coconut oil, melted
- 1/4 cup chicken broth, low sodium or your own chicken bone broth
- 1/4 cup water

Instructions
1. Preheat your oven to 350°F (175°C) and line a baking sheet with parchment paper.
2. In a large bowl, combine the cooked mixed meats, cooked peas, coconut flakes, coconut flour, melted coconut oil, chicken broth, and water. Mix well until all the ingredients are evenly incorporated.
3. Scoop out tablespoon-sized portions of the mixture and place them on the prepared baking sheet. Flatten each portion with the back of a spoon to form a small, round cookie shape.
4. Bake the treats in the preheated oven for 15-20 minutes, or until they are golden brown and firm to the touch.
5. Remove the treats from the oven and let them cool completely before serving to your dog.

32 Coconut Turkey with Organ Meats

Prepare yourself for a culinary creation that defines excellence—organ meat delights for your furry friend. Now, we're not just talking any meat; we're talking liver, heart, and kidneys—the powerhouse of nutrients that your dog craves and deserves.

Start with a pound of ground turkey; it sets the stage for a protein-packed experience. Then, in comes the trio of chicken liver, hearts, and gizzards—chopped to perfection, ensuring each bite is a symphony of flavors and textures. These organ meats aren't just a treat; they're a nutrient-rich powerhouse, providing essential vitamins and minerals for your dog's overall well-being.

To bind this masterpiece together, we add a touch of unsweetened coconut flakes, offering a subtle sweetness and a hint of tropical indulgence. Now, for the secret ingredient—coconut oil. Melted to perfection, it not only adds a richness that dogs adore but also brings a host of health benefits, from a luscious coat to a happy heart.

And, of course, a dish like this deserves a touch of sophistication. We introduce low-sodium chicken broth or, for the true connoisseur, your very own chicken bone broth. It's not just about flavor; it's about crafting a treat that's as nourishing as it is delightful.

Form these delectable portions into small, round shapes, bake until they achieve that perfect golden brown, and voilà—organ meat delights that redefine canine indulgence. Because your dog deserves nothing less than culinary excellence, and these treats deliver just that.

Ingredients
- 1 pound ground turkey
- 1/4 cup unsweetened coconut flakes
- 1/4 cup chicken liver, chopped
- 1/4 cup chicken hearts, chopped
- 1/4 cup chicken gizzards, chopped
- 1/4 cup coconut oil, melted
- 1/4 cup chicken broth, low sodium or your own chicken bone broth
- 1/4 cup water

Instructions
1. Preheat your oven to 350°F (175°C) and line a baking sheet with parchment paper.
2. In a large bowl, combine the ground turkey, coconut flakes, chopped chicken liver, chopped chicken hearts, chopped chicken gizzards, melted coconut oil, chicken broth, and water. Mix well until all the ingredients are evenly incorporated.
3. Scoop out tablespoon-sized portions of the mixture and place them on the prepared baking sheet. Flatten each portion with the back of a spoon to form a small, round cookie shape.
4. Bake the treats in the preheated oven for 15-20 minutes, or until they are golden brown and firm to the touch.
5. Remove the treats from the oven and let them cool completely before serving to your dog

Beef, Kidney, and Spinach Stew

Embark on a culinary odyssey for your discerning dog with our Beef, Kidney, and Spinach Stew—a symphony of flavors and nutrition. The beef stew meat, a protein powerhouse, dances with nutrient-rich beef kidney, ensuring a strong frame and a shining coat. Spinach, a leafy green marvel, fortifies the immune system, while coconut adds a touch of brilliance. Freeze for a lasting feast, or customize with alternatives like turkey or chicken for culinary versatility. It's not just a meal; it's a Chef Ramsey-approved experience, tailor-made for your pup's delight.

Ingredients
- 1 pound beef stew meat, cut into small pieces
- 1/2 cup beef kidney, chopped
- 1 cup fresh spinach, chopped
- 1/4 cup unsweetened coconut flakes
- 1/4 cup coconut oil, melted
- 1/4 cup chicken broth, low sodium
- 1/4 cup water

Instructions
1. In a large pot, brown the beef stew meat over medium-high heat until it is cooked through.
2. Add the chopped beef kidney to the pot and cook for an additional 5-7 minutes, or until the kidney is cooked through.
3. Add the chopped spinach, coconut flakes, melted coconut oil, chicken broth, and water to the pot. Mix well until all the ingredients are evenly incorporated.
4. Simmer the stew over low heat for 20-30 minutes, or until the spinach is wilted and the flavors have melded together.
5. Let the stew cool completely before serving to your dog.

34

Pulled Chicken and Cauliflower Mash

Indulge your pup in a gastronomic delight with our Pulled Chicken and Cauliflower Mash. Crafted with the utmost care, this recipe combines lean chicken, a protein powerhouse, with the wholesome goodness of cauliflower. Yes, you heard it right—cauliflower for canines! A low-calorie marvel rich in fiber, vitamins, and minerals. Blended with coconut for a dash of healthy fats, this dish promises not just a meal but a nutritional symphony for your furry friend. Serve it up and witness tails wag in pure delight.

Ingredients
- 1 pound boneless, skinless chicken breasts
- 1 head cauliflower, chopped into small florets
- 1/4 cup unsweetened coconut flakes
- 1/4 cup coconut oil, melted
- 1/4 cup chicken broth, low sodium or your own chicken bone broth
- 1/4 cup water

Instructions
1. Preheat your oven to 350°F (175°C) and line a baking sheet with parchment paper.
2. Place the chicken breasts on the prepared baking sheet and bake for 20-25 minutes, or until cooked through. Let them cool.
3. In a large pot, steam the cauliflower florets until they are tender.
4. In a blender or food processor, blend the steamed cauliflower until it reaches a mashed potato-like consistency.
5. Shred the cooked chicken breasts with a fork or chop them into small pieces.
6. In a mixing bowl, combine the shredded chicken, mashed cauliflower, coconut flakes, melted coconut oil, chicken broth, and water. Mix well until all the ingredients are evenly incorporated.
7. Serve the pulled chicken and cauliflower mash to your dog in a bowl.

Eggs

Elevate your dog's diet with the nutritional powerhouse of eggs! These versatile wonders bring a protein-packed punch, along with a medley of vitamins and minerals, fostering a spectrum of health benefits. From enhancing skin and coat luster to promoting robust digestion and an energetic spirit, eggs are a canine superfood.

Whether you opt for the simplicity of boiled, the fluffiness of scrambled, or the wholesome baked goodness, it's crucial to present eggs in their purest form—devoid of oils, butter, salt, or any additives. The culinary magic lies in the inherent goodness of eggs, promoting overall well-being.

However, caution is the chef's secret ingredient. Moderation is the guiding principle, with a cap of one egg per day. While the nutrient-rich profile is a boon, an excess of protein can tip the scales, potentially leading to weight gain in our furry friends.

Remember, the kitchen rulebook insists on cooking eggs for your canine companion. This not only ensures palatability but also sidesteps potential hazards like salmonella and biotin deficiency. With these culinary insights, you're poised to whip up a delightful and nutritious treat, adding a dash of egg-cellence to your dog's dining experience.

The Complicated Turkey and Green Bean Stew with Eggs

35

Indulge your buddy with our Turkey and Green Bean Stew, a culinary masterpiece crafted with love and nutrition in mind. Ground white meat turkey takes center stage, accompanied by brown rice, hard-boiled eggs, and a melody of veggies. Sweet potatoes, peas, green beans, cranberries, and a sprinkle of herbs create a symphony of flavors. Drizzle with your chosen healthy oil, and voilà–a canine delight that's both delicious and nutritious. Serve alone or mix with kibble for a culinary experience tailored to your furry friend's taste.

Ingredients
- 2 pounds ground white meat turkey, cooked thoroughly and drained
- 6 cups cooked brown rice (or white rice if your dog has a kidney disease diagnosis)
- 6 hard-boiled eggs
- 2 large sweet potatoes, scrubbed clean, peeled, cubed, and steamed
- 1 (15-ounce) bag frozen peas
- 1 (15-ounce) bag frozen green beans
- ½ cup fresh cranberries, sliced thin
- ¼ cup hemp hearts
- ¼ cup parsley
- 6 sage leaves, minced
- 3 tablespoons minced rosemary
- 3 tablespoons olive oil, Udo's omega-3 and omega-6 oil blend, or safflower oil

Instructions
1. In a large mixing bowl, combine the cooked ground turkey, cooked rice, and hard-boiled eggs. Mix well.
2. Add the steamed sweet potatoes, frozen peas, frozen green beans, cranberries, hemp hearts, parsley, sage leaves, minced rosemary, and olive oil. Mix until all ingredients are evenly distributed.
3. Portion out the stew into individual servings, based on your dog's weight and dietary needs.
4. Serve the stew to your dog, either on its own or mixed with their regular kibble.

Gizzard and Zucchini Stir Fry with Dog Safe Spices

36

Elevate your dog's dining experience with our Chicken Gizzard and Zucchini Medley—a nutritious and flavorful delight. Chicken gizzards, rich in glucosamine, vitamin B12, and protein, team up with zucchini for a well-rounded meal. Expertly seasoned with turmeric, cumin, coriander, ginger, and cinnamon, this dish not only tantalizes the taste buds but also offers health benefits. Cooked to perfection in coconut oil, it's a wholesome treat for your furry companion. Serve in moderation as a special addition to their daily routine, ensuring a balance of flavors and nutrients. Bon appétit!

Ingredients
- 1 pound chicken gizzards
- 2 medium zucchinis, sliced into thin strips
- 1 tablespoon coconut oil
- 1/2 teaspoon turmeric powder
- 1/2 teaspoon cumin powder
- 1/2 teaspoon coriander powder
- 1/2 teaspoon ginger powder
- 1/2 teaspoon cinnamon powder

Instructions
1. In a large pot, bring water to a boil and add the chicken gizzards. Cook for 1 hour or until the gizzards are tender. Drain and set aside to cool.
2. Once the gizzards are cool, use your fingers or a fork to shred them into small pieces.
3. In a large skillet, heat the coconut oil over medium heat. Add the black mustard seeds and cook until they start to pop.
4. Add the zucchini strips to the skillet and cook for 3-4 minutes, or until they start to soften.
5. In a small bowl, mix together the turmeric, cumin, coriander, ginger, and cinnamon. Add this spice mixture to the skillet and stir well to coat the zucchini.
6. Add the shredded gizzards to the skillet and cook for an additional 2-3 minutes, or until everything is heated through.
7. Remove the skillet from the heat and let the stir fry cool before serving to your dog.

Coriander and Ginger

Coriander and ginger, when incorporated in a dog's diet in moderation, can provide various health benefits. Coriander, known for its anti-nausea and detoxifying properties, can be introduced by sprinkling 1/16 to ¼ teaspoon of ground seeds or root on the dog's food. It offers potential relief for digestive issues and helps detoxify the body. On the other hand, ginger, recognized for its anti-inflammatory properties, serves as a remedy for nausea and upset stomach in dogs. The recommended dosage is 20 to 50 mg per kg of body weight, with a precautionary limit of no more than one teaspoon a day to prevent potential heartburn. However, it's crucial to consult with a veterinarian before incorporating these spices into a dog's diet, especially for dogs with underlying health conditions or those taking medication.

37 Pulled Chicken, Pea, and Yam Stew

This wholesome stew is a nutritious delight for your canine companion. Packed with vitamins A, B, C, and K from the peas, and boasting essential nutrients like protein and fiber, it provides a balanced and delicious meal. It's crucial to avoid canned peas due to their high sodium content, making fresh or frozen peas the healthier choice. In this recipe, boneless, skinless chicken breasts are cooked to perfection with a medley of peas and diced yam, creating a flavorful blend. The addition of low-sodium chicken broth enhances the taste while maintaining a healthy balance. Once cooked, shred the chicken and mix it back into the stew for a delightful canine feast. Remember to allow the stew to cool before serving, and any leftovers can be stored in the refrigerator for up to 3 days in an airtight container. Your dog is sure to savor every nutritious bite!

Ingredients:
- 2 boneless, skinless chicken breasts
- 1 cup frozen peas
- 1 medium yam, peeled and diced
- 1 cup low-sodium chicken broth or your own chicken bone broth
- 1 cup water
- 1 tablespoon olive oil

Instructions
1. In a large pot, heat the olive oil over medium heat. Add the chicken breasts and cook until browned on both sides, about 5 minutes per side.

2. Add the chicken broth, water, peas, and yam to the pot. Bring to a boil, then reduce the heat to low and simmer for 20-25 minutes, or until the chicken is cooked through and the yam is tender.

3. Remove the chicken from the pot and shred it using two forks. Return the shredded chicken to the pot and stir to combine with the peas and yam.

4. Allow the stew to cool before serving it to your dog. Store any leftovers in an airtight container in the refrigerator for up to 3 days.

Vegetable Stew with Organ Meats

38

Indulge your furry friend in a nutrient-packed delight with this Vegetable Stew featuring beef liver and kidney. Recognized as canine superfoods, these organs provide a wealth of vitamins A, B, and D, along with essential fatty acids, iron, copper, and zinc. This powerful combination supports healthy bones, joints, digestion, immune function, and vision. The inclusion of mixed vegetables such as carrots, green beans, peas, and sweet potatoes adds a flavorful and wholesome touch. The stew is further enriched with low-sodium beef broth, ensuring a well-balanced and delicious meal for your dog. As with any new addition to their diet, moderation is key to prevent digestive upset, and consulting with your veterinarian is advised. After preparing this hearty stew, allow it to cool before serving, and any leftovers can be stored in the refrigerator for up to 3 days. Treat your canine companion to the goodness they deserve!

Ingredients
- 1 pound beef liver, chopped
- 1 pound beef kidney, chopped
- 2 cups mixed vegetables (carrots, green beans, peas, sweet potatoes)
- 1 cup low-sodium beef broth or your own bone broth
- 1 cup water
- 1 tablespoon olive oil

Instructions
1. In a large pot, heat the olive oil over medium heat. Add the chopped liver and kidney and cook until browned on all sides, about 5 minutes.
2. Add the mixed vegetables, beef broth, and water to the pot. Bring to a boil, then reduce the heat to low and simmer for 20-25 minutes, or until the vegetables are tender and the organ meats are cooked through.
3. Allow the stew to cool before serving it to your dog. Store any leftovers in an airtight container in the refrigerator for up to 3 days.

Sweet Potato Bake with Inexpensive Cut of Beef

Treat your dog to a delightful and nutritious Sweet Potato Bake that can be crafted with an inexpensive cut of beef, offering a budget-friendly yet flavorful option. Sliced into thin strips, the beef is quickly browned to perfection in olive oil, providing a savory touch to the dish. Paired with sweet potato rounds, the layers are artfully arranged in a baking dish, creating a visually appealing and wholesome meal. A generous cup of low-sodium beef broth or your homemade bone broth is poured over the layers, infusing the bake with additional moisture and flavor. Covered with foil, the dish is baked until the sweet potatoes reach a tender consistency and the beef is thoroughly cooked. After allowing it to cool, your dog can enjoy this delicious creation, and any leftovers can be stored in the refrigerator for up to 3 days. This simple yet satisfying recipe ensures your canine companion receives a well-balanced and tasty treat.

Ingredients
- 1 pound inexpensive cut of beef, sliced into thin strips
- 2 medium sweet potatoes, peeled and sliced into thin rounds
- 1 cup low-sodium beef broth or your own bone broth
- 1 tablespoon olive oil

Instructions
1. Preheat the oven to 375°F.
2. In a large skillet, heat the olive oil over medium heat. Add the beef strips and cook until browned on all sides, about 5 minutes.
3. In a large baking dish, layer the sweet potato rounds and beef strips, alternating between the two.
4. Pour the beef broth over the sweet potato and beef layers.
5. Cover the baking dish with foil and bake for 45-50 minutes, or until the sweet potatoes are tender and the beef is cooked through.
6. Allow the sweet potato bake to cool before serving it to your dog. Store any leftovers in an airtight container in the refrigerator for up to 3 days.

40

Chicken and Rice Casserole

Indulge your canine companion with a delectable and wholesome Chicken and Brown Rice Casserole, specially crafted for a gentle and nourishing experience. Begin by sautéing boneless, skinless chicken pieces in olive oil until they achieve a delightful golden brown. Incorporate uncooked brown rice, low-sodium chicken broth or your homemade bone broth, and a medley of mixed vegetables such as carrots, green beans, and peas into the pot. Bring this harmonious blend to a boil and simmer until the rice is tender and the vegetables reach optimal tenderness. Transfer the flavorful chicken and rice concoction to a spacious baking dish, cover it with foil, and bake until heated through. After allowing the casserole to cool, your furry friend can savor this delightful creation. Any leftovers can be conveniently stored in an airtight container in the refrigerator for up to 3 days. This recipe ensures your dog receives a balanced and scrumptious meal, making mealtime a joyful experience.

Ingredients
- 1 pound boneless, skinless chicken breasts, cut into small pieces
- 1 cup uncooked brown rice
- 2 cups low-sodium chicken broth or your own bone broth
- 1 cup mixed vegetables (carrots, green beans, peas)
- 1 tablespoon olive oil

Instructions
1. Preheat the oven to 375°F.
2. In a large pot, heat the olive oil over medium heat. Add the chicken pieces and cook until browned on all sides, about 5 minutes.
3. Add the brown rice, chicken broth, and mixed vegetables to the pot. Bring to a boil, then reduce the heat to low and simmer for 20-25 minutes, or until the rice is cooked and the vegetables are tender.
4. Transfer the chicken and rice mixture to a large baking dish. Cover with foil and bake for 20-25 minutes, or until heated through.
5. Allow the casserole to cool before serving it to your dog. Store any leftovers in an airtight container in the refrigerator for up to 3 days.

41

Beef and Sweet Potato Casserole

Elevate your dog's dining experience with the delectable Beef and Sweet Potato Casserole – a harmonious blend of flavors and nutrients crafted to perfection. Begin by browning lean ground beef in olive oil, creating a savory foundation for this culinary delight. Add diced sweet potatoes and chopped green beans to the mix, allowing them to infuse their wholesome goodness into the dish. Pour in low-sodium beef broth or your homemade bone broth to enhance the richness of the casserole. Transfer this delectable medley to a spacious baking dish, cover it with foil, and bake until the sweet potatoes achieve a tender perfection. After allowing the casserole to cool, your furry friend can relish this nourishing creation. Store any remaining portions in an airtight container in the refrigerator for up to 3 days. This recipe ensures that each bite is a delightful balance of protein, carbohydrates, and fiber, making mealtime a joyous occasion for your cherished pet.

Ingredients
- 1 pound lean ground beef
- 2 medium sweet potatoes, peeled and diced
- 1 cup green beans, chopped
- 1 cup low-sodium beef broth or your own bone broth
- 1 tablespoon olive oil

Instructions
1. Preheat the oven to 375°F.
2. In a large skillet, heat the olive oil over medium heat. Add the ground beef and cook until browned, about 5-7 minutes.
3. Add the sweet potatoes and green beans to the skillet and cook for an additional 5 minutes, or until the vegetables are slightly softened.
4. Transfer the beef and vegetable mixture to a large baking dish. Pour the beef broth over the top.
5. Cover the baking dish with foil and bake for 30-35 minutes, or until the sweet potatoes are tender and the beef is cooked through.
6. Allow the casserole to cool before serving it to your dog. Store any leftovers in an airtight container in the refrigerator for up to 3 days.

42

Turkey and Quinoa Casserole

Delight your dog's taste buds with the wholesome goodness of the Turkey and Quinoa Casserole. This delectable dish features the nutritious benefits of quinoa, a pseudo-cereal known for its protein, fiber, and rich array of vitamins and minerals. Begin by combining ground white meat turkey, cooked quinoa, a medley of mixed vegetables, fresh parsley, an egg, and a touch of olive oil in a mixing bowl. Stir the ingredients until they harmonize into a delectable ensemble. Transfer this delightful mixture into a casserole dish, then let it bake in the preheated oven until it reaches a perfect, savory completion. Allow the casserole to cool to room temperature before presenting it to your beloved canine companion. With each bite, your furry friend will savor the balanced flavors and nourishing elements of this thoughtfully crafted Turkey and Quinoa Casserole, ensuring a mealtime experience filled with joy and wellness.

Ingredients
- 1 pound ground white meat turkey
- 1 cup cooked quinoa
- 1/2 cup mixed vegetables (such as carrots, green beans, and sweet potatoes)
- 1/4 cup fresh parsley
- 1 egg
- 1 tablespoon olive oil

Instructions
1. Preheat the oven to 350°F.
2. In a large mixing bowl, combine the ground white meat turkey, cooked quinoa, mixed vegetables, fresh parsley, egg, and olive oil.
3. Mix all the ingredients together until well combined.
4. Pour the mixture into a casserole dish.
5. Bake the casserole in the preheated oven for 30-35 minutes, or until cooked through.
6. Let the casserole cool to room temperature before serving to your dog.

Quinoa

Discover the nutritional wonders of quinoa, a safe and beneficial addition to your dog's diet:

1. Rich in Protein, Fiber, and Essential Fatty Acids: Quinoa provides a wholesome combination of protein, fiber, and essential fatty acids, promoting optimal digestive health and a satisfying feeling for your furry friend.

2. Gluten-Free Goodness: Being gluten-free, quinoa serves as an excellent choice for dogs with sensitivities or allergies to gluten-containing grains like wheat, corn, or rice.

3. Antioxidant Powerhouse: Packed with antioxidants such as flavonoids, quercetin, and kaempferol, quinoa aids in reducing inflammation and may contribute to preventing diseases like cancer.

4. Essential Nutrients: Quinoa delivers essential B-vitamins, magnesium, and iron, supporting your dog's overall health and well-being.

5. Grain Sensitivity Solution: Often used as a grain substitute, quinoa is a suitable option for dogs with sensitivities to traditional grains, offering a nutritious alternative.

As you introduce quinoa to your dog's diet, do so gradually and in moderation. If you have any concerns about your dog's health or dietary needs, consulting with your veterinarian is always a wise choice. Elevate your pet's nutrition with the wholesome benefits of quinoa!

Salmon

Incorporating salmon into your dog's diet can offer a plethora of nutritional benefits, contributing to their overall health and well-being. Here's a closer look at why salmon is considered a valuable addition:

1. Protein Powerhouse: Salmon is renowned for its rich protein content, playing a pivotal role in supporting your dog's muscle development and overall strength.

2. Omega-3 Fatty Acids: Abundant in omega-3 fatty acids, salmon provides vital nutrients that promote improved skin and coat health. These fatty acids also contribute to reducing inflammation, enhancing your dog's mobility and promoting a healthy heart.

3. Vitamin and Mineral Bounty: Packed with essential vitamins and minerals, including B vitamins and selenium, salmon offers a well-rounded nutritional profile. This can positively impact your dog's immune system, energy levels, and various physiological functions.

4. Salmon's Role in Disease Prevention: The omega-3 fatty acids in salmon contribute to overall disease prevention, supporting conditions such as arthritis and promoting cognitive health in senior dogs.

5. Cautionary Notes: While salmon is highly beneficial, caution must be exercised. Raw or undercooked salmon should be avoided due to the potential presence of parasites that can lead to salmon poisoning disease. To ensure the optimal incorporation of salmon into your dog's diet, it's advisable to consult with your veterinarian. This is particularly crucial if your dog has pre-existing health conditions or is currently on medication.

In summary, the inclusion of salmon in your dog's diet, when done in moderation and as part of a balanced nutrition plan, can serve as a delicious and nutritious way to enhance their overall health.'

43 Salmon and Sweet Potato Casserole

Indulge your canine companion with a nutritious and flavorful treat by preparing this Salmon and Sweet Potato Casserole. Packed with omega-3 fatty acids and fiber, this dish contributes to your dog's overall well-being. Here's how to create this wholesome casserole:

Ingredients:
- 1 pound cooked salmon, flaked
- 2 medium sweet potatoes, peeled and diced
- 1 cup green beans, chopped
- 1 cup low-sodium chicken broth
- 1 tablespoon olive oil

Instructions:
1. Preheat the Oven: Set your oven to 375°F to prepare for baking.
2. Mix the Ingredients: In a spacious bowl, combine the flaked salmon, diced sweet potatoes, and chopped green beans.
3. Transfer to Baking Dish: Place the salmon and vegetable mixture into a generously sized baking dish.
4. Add Chicken Broth: Pour the low-sodium chicken broth evenly over the ingredients in the baking dish.
5. Bake to Perfection: Cover the baking dish with foil and bake for 20-25 minutes, ensuring it's heated through.
6. Cool and Serve: Allow the casserole to cool before serving it to your dog. This ensures a safe and enjoyable dining experience.
7. Storage: Any leftovers can be stored in an airtight container in the refrigerator for up to 3 days.

Spoil your furry friend with this delectable casserole, providing a delightful combination of flavors and essential nutrients. Always ensure that the ingredients align with your dog's dietary needs, and consult with your veterinarian for personalized advice.

44 Lamb and Barley Casserole

Elevate your dog's dining experience with this Lamb and Barley Casserole, a wholesome combination of high-quality protein and essential nutrients. Here's how you can prepare this nutrition-packed dish:

Ingredients:
- 1 pound ground lamb
- 1 cup cooked barley
- 1 cup cooked carrots, mashed
- 1 cup cooked peas
- 1/2 cup low-sodium chicken broth
- 1/4 cup chopped fresh parsley

Instructions:
1. Preheat the Oven: Set your oven to 350°F (175°C) to prepare for baking.
2. Cook the Lamb: In a large skillet, cook the ground lamb over medium heat until browned and fully cooked. Drain any excess fat.
3. Mix the Ingredients: In a spacious mixing bowl, combine the cooked lamb, barley, mashed carrots, peas, low-sodium chicken broth, and chopped parsley. Ensure thorough mixing to combine all the ingredients.
4. Transfer to Casserole Dish: Spread the mixture evenly in a casserole dish.
5. Bake to Perfection: Place the casserole in the preheated oven and bake for 20-25 minutes until heated through, with a slightly browned top.
6. Cool Before Serving: Allow the casserole to cool completely before serving it to your dog. For convenient storage, divide it into single servings and freeze them for later use.

Optimize your dog's nutrition with the richness of lamb, barley, and wholesome vegetables. Before introducing any new elements to your dog's diet, consult your veterinarian for personalized advice and ensure the recipe aligns with your dog's specific needs.'

Ancient Grains

Ancient grains, renowned for their safety and nutritional value, offer various health advantages for dogs:

- Abundant in protein and fiber, these grains contribute to your dog's digestive well-being, promoting satiety and fullness.

- Packed with prebiotics, ancient grains foster the growth of beneficial gut bacteria, fortifying your dog's immune system.

- Rich in essential vitamins and minerals like iron, magnesium, and zinc, ancient grains contribute to your dog's overall health and vitality.

- Compared to common grains like wheat and corn, ancient grains are less likely to trigger food sensitivities or allergies in dogs.

It's crucial to recognize that the nutritional composition can vary among ancient grains. When introducing these grains into your dog's diet, a gradual and moderate approach is recommended. Consulting with your veterinarian ensures that you tailor your dog's diet to meet their specific health needs and concerns.

Grass-Fed Beef and Ancient Grains

45

Crafted with nutritious ingredients like grass-fed beef, brown rice, pearled barley, oatmeal, quinoa, millet, and wholesome vegetables, this recipe forms a well-balanced and nourishing meal for your dog.

Ingredients
- 1 pound grass-fed beef
- 1 cup cooked brown rice
- 1 cup cooked pearled barley
- 1 cup cooked oatmeal
- 1/2 cup cooked quinoa
- 1/2 cup cooked millet
- 1/2 cup mixed vegetables (carrots, green beans, peas)
- 1 tablespoon olive oil

Instructions
1. Preheat the oven to 375°F.
2. In a large skillet, heat the olive oil over medium heat, adding the ground beef and cooking until browned, approximately 5-7 minutes.
3. In a spacious mixing bowl, blend the cooked brown rice, pearled barley, oatmeal, quinoa, millet, and mixed vegetables, ensuring an even distribution of ingredients.
4. Integrate the cooked ground beef into the mixture, stirring thoroughly.
5. Transfer the amalgam to a casserole dish, spreading it out uniformly.
6. Bake the casserole in the preheated oven for 20-25 minutes until heated through and the top achieves a slight browning.
7. Allow the casserole to cool completely before serving it to your dog. You can portion it into individual servings and freeze them for future use.'

Cage-Free Chicken and Ancient Grains Recipe for Small Breed Dogs

46

Crafted with utmost care, this recipe features succulent cage-free chicken harmoniously blended with wholesome ingredients like brown rice, pearled barley, oatmeal, quinoa, millet, and a medley of dog-friendly vegetables. It's a meticulously crafted, balanced, and nourishing meal tailored for the discerning taste buds of small breed dogs.

Ingredients:
- 1 pound cage-free chicken
- 1 cup cooked brown rice
- 1 cup cooked pearled barley
- 1 cup cooked oatmeal
- 1/2 cup cooked quinoa
- 1/2 cup cooked millet
- 1/2 cup mixed vegetables (carrots, green beans, peas)
- 1 tablespoon olive oil

Instructions:
1. Preheat the oven to 375°F.
2. In a generous skillet, infuse the olive oil over medium heat. Introduce the chicken, ensuring a golden brown sear for about 5-7 minutes.
3. In a capacious mixing bowl, orchestrate a symphony of cooked brown rice, pearled barley, oatmeal, quinoa, millet, and the vibrant vegetable ensemble. Ensure a harmonious blend of all constituents.
4. Mingle the cooked chicken into the orchestrated concerto within the mixing bowl, creating a delightful composition.
5. Stage the culinary masterpiece in a casserole dish, spreading it evenly to capture the essence of each element.
6. Allow the casserole to grace the oven's stage for 20-25 minutes, attaining a crescendo of flavors until the top achieves a symphony of slight browning.
7. Let the culinary opus cool gracefully before presenting it to your petite companion. Consider dividing it into single servings, freezing them for future culinary encores.

The Salmon, Catfish, and Oats Bowl

47

In the realm of doggy dining, behold the extraordinary infusion of omega-3 fatty acids, where the illustrious catfish takes center stage. Not merely a savory protein source, catfish is a virtuoso of essential nutrients, generously endowing your canine companion with iron, proteins, and the dynamic duo of vitamins A and B12. As we embark on this gastronomic journey, envision a culinary masterpiece that not only tantalizes taste buds but also nurtures your dog's holistic well-being.

Ingredients:
- 1/2 cup old-fashioned rolled oats
- 1/2 pound salmon fillet, skin removed
- 1/2 pound catfish fillet, skin removed
- Water

Instructions:
1. In the culinary theater preheated to 350°F, let the curtains rise on our gastronomic opus.
2. Conduct the oats in a melodic crescendo, orchestrating a harmonious symphony of flavors, cooked to perfection with water as the instrumental medium.
3. As the oats cool, let the salmon and catfish grace the stage, their skins ceremoniously removed, ready to dance in bite-sized ecstasy.
4. In the grand mixing bowl, let the ensemble of cooked oats, salmon, and catfish engage in a ballet of flavors, each movement carefully choreographed.
5. With a maestro's touch, blend the elements until they sing in unison, an edible sonnet of health and indulgence.
6. In the silicone muffin pan, let each cup become a stage, cradling the composition, filling the air with anticipation.
7. Bake this culinary crescendo for 20-25 minutes, witnessing the transformation as the fish becomes a golden brown crescendo.
8. As the masterpiece cools, it awaits its grand finale, a presentation to your loyal audience – your canine connoisseur. May this symphony of flavors elevate your dog's dining experience to a crescendo of delight and well-being.

Chicken Vegetable Soup

Simplicity itself.

48

Ingredients
- 2 boneless, skinless chicken breasts
- 1 cup chopped carrots
- 1 cup chopped celery
- 1 cup chopped sweet potato
- 1 cup chopped green beans
- 6 cups water or bone broth for dogs
- 1 teaspoon dog-safe herbs (optional)

Instructions
1. In a large pot, combine the chicken breasts, carrots, celery, sweet potato, green beans, water or bone broth, and dog-safe herbs (if using).
2. Bring the mixture to a boil over medium-high heat, then reduce the heat to low and simmer for 1 hour, or until the chicken is cooked through and the vegetables are tender.
3. Remove the chicken breasts from the pot and shred them using two forks. Return the shredded chicken to the pot and stir to combine.
4. Allow the soup to cool completely before serving to your dog. You can serve it as is or puree the vegetables for dogs that have trouble chewing.
5. To freeze the leftovers, portion the soup into airtight containers or zip-top bags and label them with the date. Freeze for up to 3 months. Thaw in the refrigerator overnight before serving to your dog.

The soup can be served as a meal on its own or as a topper for your dog's regular kibble.

Chicken and Pea Sausages

49

Embark on a culinary adventure as we craft a delectable symphony of flavors in the form of homemade sausages for your discerning canine palate.

Ingredients:

- 2 pounds ground chicken
- 1 cup frozen peas
- 1/2 cup rolled oats
- 1/4 cup chopped fresh parsley
- 1/4 cup chopped fresh mint
- 1 egg
- 1 teaspoon dog-safe herbs (optional)

Instructions:
1. The overture begins at 350°F, as the stage is set for our culinary creation.
2. In a grand mixing bowl, unite the ground chicken, frozen peas, rolled oats, parsley, mint, egg, and, should you desire, the optional symphony of dog-safe herbs.
3. A crescendo of flavors emerges as you mix the ensemble to harmonious perfection.
4. The spotlight now shines on 16 portions, each shaped into a sausage, a testament to the artisanal craftsmanship at play.
5. The sausages, poised for their debut, grace a parchment-lined baking sheet, ready to enchant the senses.
6. The stage transforms into an oven, a culinary arena where the sausages perform their alchemy for 25-30 minutes, achieving a crescendo of golden brown perfection.
7. As the applause fades, the sausages await their grand finale, a complete cool-down before gracing your dog's dining stage.
8. For an encore, freeze these masterpieces in airtight containers or zip-top bags, labeled with the date, offering a symphony of flavors for up to 3 months. Let the anticipation build as you thaw them in the refrigerator overnight, preparing for the next culinary masterpiece for your cherished canine.

50 Chicken Livers with Oats + Mint

Now, let's dive into the creation of a sensational dish that not only tantalizes your dog's taste buds but also incorporates a touch of sophistication through the inclusion of mint.

Introduction to Mint's Nutritional Symphony:
Mint, a botanical virtuoso, graces this dish with a rich ensemble of vitamins A and C, minerals such as calcium, copper, iron, and folate, all harmoniously combined with the healthful charm of fiber. Beyond its nutritional prowess, mint contributes to breath freshness, acts as a flea deterrent, and provides soothing relief to an upset stomach.

Note of Caution: While we savor the goodness of mint, let us be mindful of the toxic Pennyroyal Mint and the potential hazards posed by artificial forms like breath mints containing xylitol. As with any ingredient, moderation is key to avoid potential stomach issues in our beloved companions.

Ingredients
- 1 pound chicken livers
- 1 cup frozen peas
- 1/2 cup rolled oats
- 1/4 cup chopped fresh parsley
- 1/4 cup chopped fresh mint
- 1 egg
- 1 teaspoon dog-safe herbs (optional)

Instructions
1. In a medium-sized pot, add cleaned chicken livers and about an inch of water, then place on the stove over high heat. Once boiling, reduce the heat to a light boil for about 10-15 minutes. Don't add any additional seasoning or ingredients- the livers will taste great to your dog all by themselves.
2. After being lightly boiled for 15 minutes, turn off the heat and drain the water from the livers using a colander.
3. Let the livers cool to room temperature on a plate before moving on to the next step.
4. In a large mixing bowl, combine the cooked chicken livers, frozen peas, rolled oats, parsley, mint, egg, and dog-safe herbs (if using).
5. Mix well to combine.
6. Divide the mixture into 16 equal portions and shape each portion into a sausage shape.
7. Place the sausages on a baking sheet lined with parchment paper.
8. Bake for 25-30 minutes, or until the sausages are cooked through and golden brown.
9. Allow the sausages to cool completely before serving to your dog.

Beef, Kidney and Ancient Grains Burger

51

Ladies and gentlemen, welcome to a culinary adventure fit for your four-legged friends – the Beef, Kidney, and Ancient Grains Burger! This delectable recipe showcases the finest ingredients, including finely chopped beef kidney, ground beef, and a wholesome blend of ancient grains like quinoa, farro, or barley. Paired with vibrant frozen peas, fresh parsley, mint, and a hint of optional dog-safe herbs, this burger is a canine sensation. Each patty is a symphony of flavors, offering your furry companion a nutritious and delicious treat. Cooked to perfection in a non-stick skillet, these burgers are a fantastic addition to your dog's diet, served on their own or atop whole wheat buns for an extra touch. Remember, this culinary delight is meticulously crafted to ensure a safe and delightful experience for your furry friend, free from harmful ingredients. Let the feast begin!

Ingredients
- 1/2 pound beef kidney, finely chopped
- 1/2 pound ground beef
- 1 cup cooked ancient grains (such as quinoa, farro, or barley)
- 1/2 cup frozen peas
- 1/4 cup chopped fresh parsley
- 1/4 cup chopped fresh mint
- 1 egg
- 1 teaspoon dog-safe herbs (optional)
- Whole wheat buns (optional)

Instructions
1. In a large mixing bowl, combine the finely chopped beef, kidney, cooked ancient grains, frozen peas, parsley, mint, egg, and dog-safe herbs (if using).
2. Mix well to combine.
3. Divide the mixture into 4 equal portions and shape each portion into a burger patty.
4. Heat a non-stick skillet over medium heat and add a small amount of oil.
5. Cook the burger patties for 5-7 minutes on each side, or until they are cooked through and golden brown.
6. Allow the burgers to cool completely before serving to your dog.
7. You can serve the burgers on whole wheat buns if desired, but make sure to avoid any toppings that are toxic or harmful to dogs (such as onions or garlic).
8. To freeze the leftovers, place the burgers in airtight containers or zip-top bags and label them with the date. Freeze for up to 3 months. Thaw in the refrigerator overnight before serving to your dog.

HERBS GENERALLY CONSIDERED SAFE FOR DOGS: A PARTIAL LIST

1. Anise: While anise can have a stimulating effect on dogs in moderation, excessive amounts should be avoided due to its potent nature. It is essential to strike a balance to harness its benefits without overwhelming your canine companion.

2. Basil: Beyond adding flavor, basil boasts anti-inflammatory properties and aids in regulating blood sugar levels. Its versatility extends to providing support for memory function and combating feelings of depression in dogs.

3. Chamomile: Recognized for its calming effects, chamomile offers a trifecta of benefits, influencing muscles, skin, and digestion. This herb becomes a valuable ally for promoting relaxation and addressing various health concerns.

4. Dandelion: With its liver and gallbladder support, dandelion emerges as a powerhouse herb. Acting as a gentle diuretic, it proves particularly useful for dogs dealing with heart issues or urinary tract infections, offering a safe and effective solution.

5. Dill: Beyond enhancing breath freshness, dill lends support to the liver and pancreas. Abundant in antioxidants, it contributes to your dog's overall health, providing protective benefits against oxidative stress.

6. Rosemary: Renowned for its antimicrobial properties, rosemary not only serves as a natural preservative in dog food but also demonstrates potential in fighting common food bacteria. Its antispasmodic qualities contribute to heart health, making it a versatile herb in promoting overall cardiovascular well-being.

7. Turmeric: Celebrated for its diverse benefits, turmeric plays a pivotal role in maintaining healthy cartilage and connective tissue. Its anti-inflammatory prowess helps alleviate occasional joint stiffness and supports a balanced inflammatory response. Rich in antioxidants, turmeric aids in neutralizing free radicals, contributing to long-term health, and shows promise as a natural remedy for conditions ranging from arthritis to allergies and even cancer.

Remember, prior consultation with a veterinarian is crucial before introducing any herbs or spices into your dog's diet, ensuring a tailored approach to their well-being. Following veterinarian guidelines, especially when utilizing manufactured supplements, is essential for the optimal and safe integration of herbs into your dog's nutrition.

Bone Broth Brown Rice and Vegetable Soup

52

Very simple.

Ingredients
- 1 cup bone broth
- 1/2 cup cooked brown rice
- 1/2 cup mixed vegetables (such as carrots, green beans, and sweet potatoes)
- 1/4 cup chopped fresh parsley

Instructions
1. In a medium saucepan, bring the bone broth to a boil.
2. Add the cooked brown rice and mixed vegetables to the saucepan.
3. Reduce the heat to low and let the soup simmer for 10-15 minutes, or until the vegetables are tender.
4. Remove the saucepan from the heat and stir in the chopped parsley.
5. Let the soup cool to room temperature before serving to your dog.

Easy Freeze Turkey and Ancient Grain Balls

Introducing the "Easy Freeze Turkey and Ancient Grain Balls"—the culinary shortcut to canine delight! This recipe is not just super simple; it's a taste explosion waiting to happen. Picture this: lean ground turkey, ancient grains like quinoa or farro, a symphony of mixed vegetables, and a dash of fresh parsley, all mingling in perfect harmony. But the real magic? They're transformed into delightful bite-sized balls, baked to golden perfection, and ready to be devoured by your furry friend. Is it a treat? Absolutely. Is it a meal? You bet. These little wonders are the versatile answer to your dog's culinary cravings, effortlessly frozen for future feasting. From treat time to mealtime, this recipe is canine cuisine at its easiest and most enjoyable. Prepare for tails to wag and taste buds to dance—because every ball is a burst of joy for your fur companion!

Ingredients
- 1 pound ground turkey
- 1 cup cooked ancient grains (such as quinoa or farro)
- 1/2 cup mixed vegetables (such as carrots, green beans, and sweet potatoes)
- 1/4 cup chopped fresh parsley
- 1 egg
- 1 tablespoon olive oil

Instructions
1. Preheat the oven to 350°F.
2. In a large mixing bowl, combine the ground turkey, cooked ancient grains, mixed vegetables, chopped parsley, egg, and olive oil.
3. Mix all the ingredients together until well combined.
4. Form the mixture into small balls, about the size of a golf ball.
5. Place the balls on a baking sheet lined with parchment paper.
6. Bake the balls in the preheated oven for 20-25 minutes, or until cooked through.
7. Let the balls cool to room temperature before freezing.
8. To freeze, place the balls in an airtight container or freezer bag and store in the freezer for up to 3 months.
9. To thaw, remove the desired number of balls from the freezer and let them thaw in the refrigerator overnight.
10. Once thawed, the balls can be served as a meal or used as a treat.

Easy Freeze Mixed-Game and Barley Balls

An easy, pleasing recipe in a fun format.

52C

BONUS!

Ladies and gentlemen, presenting the grand finale of our culinary journey for our beloved canine companions—the "Easy Freeze Mixed-Game and Barley Balls." In this extraordinary creation, we bring together the richness of mixed game meats, including the majestic flavors of venison, elk, or bison, blended harmoniously with the wholesome goodness of cooked barley, vibrant mixed vegetables, fresh parsley, and a touch of olive oil. This culinary masterpiece is not just a meal; it's an experience—a joyous fusion of textures and flavors that dance on the palate of your cherished canine friend. But the magic doesn't stop there. Shaped into delightful balls and baked to perfection, these culinary gems are not only a feast for the senses but also a practical treat, easily frozen to ensure a supply of canine bliss for up to three months. To thaw is to anticipate, and once revealed, these savory delights can be offered as a complete meal or enjoyed as a reward—a testament to the delight we strive to provide for our faithful companions.
Bon appétit, furry friends!

Ingredients
- 1 pound mixed game meat (such as venison, elk, or bison)
- 1 cup cooked barley
- 1/2 cup mixed vegetables (such as carrots, green beans, and sweet potatoes)
- 1/4 cup chopped fresh parsley
- 1 egg
- 1 tablespoon olive oil

Instructions
1. Preheat the oven to 350°F.
2. In a large mixing bowl, combine the mixed game meat, cooked barley, mixed vegetables, chopped parsley, egg, and olive oil.
3. Mix all the ingredients together until well combined.
4. Form the mixture into small balls, about the size of a golf ball.
5. Place the balls on a baking sheet lined with parchment paper.
6. Bake the balls in the preheated oven for 20-25 minutes, or until cooked through.
7. Let the balls cool to room temperature before freezing.
8. To freeze, place the balls in an airtight container or freezer bag and store in the freezer for up to 3 months.
9. To thaw, remove the desired number of balls from the freezer and let them thaw in the refrigerator overnight.
10. Once thawed, the balls can be served as a meal or used as a treat.

PEANUT BUTTER

Listen up! Paying attention to what your dog consumes is crucial, especially when it comes to something as seemingly innocent as peanut butter.

Now, not all peanut butter is created equal, and you need to be the vigilant gatekeeper of your canine companion's diet. While peanut butter, in moderation, can offer some health benefits like protein and healthy fats, don't be fooled into thinking any jar off the shelf is safe. The devil's in the details, or in this case, the ingredients. Steer clear of peanut butter with xylitol—a canine nightmare that can be downright toxic. And let's not forget those impostors loaded with excess sodium, sugar, or additives; they're a big no-no.

Opt for the healthiest choices like unsalted peanut butter, dog-specific peanut butter, or whip up a homemade batch free from unnecessary extras. But here's the drill: moderation is key. Peanut butter is a treat, not a meal replacement.

So, next time you're reaching for that jar, read the label, stick to the guidelines, and consult your veterinarian if in doubt. And if you're wondering about the best brands for your pup, think Whole Foods' 365, Teddie Super Chunky, or Poochie Peanut Butter—simple, safe, and tail-waggingly tasty. Remember, it's your responsibility to make those peanut butter choices count for your furry friend's health.

8 DOG-SAFE TREATS, GRAVIES AND CAKES

Here Are 5 Bone Broth Treat Ideas That Are Dog Safe

Alright, listen up, pet parents! We're diving into the world of dog treats, and I've got five bone broth-infused ideas that will have your furry friend wagging their tail in delight.

First up, we've got Frozen Bone Broth Treats—pour that liquid gold into ice cube trays, freeze 'em up, and boom, you've got a refreshing snack for those scorching days.

Next, Bone Broth Popsicles. Mix bone broth with yogurt, freeze in cube trays, and watch your pup indulge in a frosty, healthy delight.

Now, who doesn't love a good gummy? Introducing Bone Broth Gummies—mix with gelatin, set in a silicone mold, and you've got yourself a chewy, nutritious treat.

Feeling a bit more traditional? How about Bone Broth Biscuits? Flour, oats, egg, and, of course, bone broth, baked to crunchy perfection.

And for the grand finale, Bone Broth Gravy! Mix it with tapioca flour and drizzle it over your pup's meal for a tasty, nutritious upgrade. Bone broth just became the VIP of your dog's treat world—simple, delicious, and packed with all the good stuff. Get in that kitchen and treat your four-legged friend to something special!

The Gummies and Biscuits are both odd-recipes-out. Let's take a look at how we make those...

Making bone broth gummies for your furry friend is a breeze.
Here's a quick and easy guide:

Bone Broth Gummies

Ingredients:
- Bone broth
- Gelatin

Instructions:
1. Heat bone broth in a saucepan on low heat. Make sure it's warm but not boiling.
2. In a separate bowl, sprinkle gelatin evenly over the bone broth. Let it sit for a minute to bloom.
3. Whisk the mixture until the gelatin is fully dissolved.
4. Pour the mixture into a silicone mold of your choice.
5. Refrigerate the mold until the gummies are set (usually a few hours or overnight).
6. Pop those gummies out of the mold, and voila – you've got yourself some bone broth-infused treats for your pup!

Remember, moderation is key, and it's always a good idea to check with your vet if you're introducing new treats into your dog's diet. Enjoy treating your furry friend!

And, here's a simple guide to making delicious bone broth biscuits for your furry companion:

Bone Broth Biscuits

Ingredients:
- Bone broth
- Flour (whole wheat or another dog-friendly alternative)
- Oats
- Egg

Instructions:
1. Preheat your oven to 350°F (175°C).
2. In a bowl, combine bone broth, flour, oats, and an egg. Adjust the quantities until you achieve a dough-like consistency.
3. Roll out the dough on a floured surface to your desired thickness.
4. Use cookie cutters to cut out shapes or simply slice the dough into squares if you prefer.
5. Place the cut shapes onto a baking sheet lined with parchment paper.
6. Bake in the preheated oven for about 15-20 minutes, or until the biscuits are golden brown.
7. Allow the bone broth biscuits to cool completely before serving them to your pup.

These homemade biscuits with the goodness of bone broth will surely become a favorite treat for your furry friend. As always, introduce new treats gradually and consult with your vet if you have any concerns about your dog's diet. Enjoy baking!

Here Are 5 Bone Broth Gravy Ideas That Are Dog Safe

Elevate your dog's dining experience with these delectable bone broth gravy ideas that not only add a burst of flavor but also pack a nutritional punch. Bone broth is a canine favorite known for its rich nutrients, and when transformed into gravy, it becomes a versatile and wholesome addition to your pup's meals. These recipes are tailor-made for our furry friends, ensuring a safe and delightful culinary experience. Whether you opt for classic chicken or turkey, introduce a medley of veggies, or explore the heartiness of lamb, these bone broth gravies are simple to prepare and guaranteed to leave your dog's tail wagging with delight. Let's dive into the world of canine culinary excellence!

1. Chicken or Turkey Gravy: Mix 1 pound of ground low-fat chicken or turkey with 2 tablespoons of cornstarch or tapioca flour and 2 cups of sodium-free or homemade stock or broth. Cook over medium heat until thickened.

2. Chicken and Vegetable Gravy: In a saucepan, heat 1 tablespoon of coconut oil and add 1 pound of ground chicken, 1/4 cup of chopped carrots, and 1/4 cup of frozen green peas. Cook until the chicken is browned. Add 3 cups of chicken stock and 2 tablespoons of cornstarch. Cook until thickened.

3. Bone Broth Gravy: In a saucepan, heat 32 ounces of homemade bone broth and 1/2 cup of organic coconut oil. Cook until the mixture is hot. Add 1 cup of organic ground turkey or chicken and cook until browned. Add 1/2 cup of tapioca flour and cook until thickened.

4. Kibble Gravy: Mix one cup of bone broth or chicken stock (no onions or garlic, please) with 2 tablespoons of arrowroot and 2 tablespoons of cool water. Cook over medium heat until thickened.

5. Lamb Gravy: Mix shredded lamb with bone broth and cook over medium heat until the mixture is hot. Add 1/2 cup of tapioca flour and cook until thickened.

Dog-Safe Cakes

Treating your furry friend to a delightful cake isn't just about celebrating special moments; it's a gesture of love and care. Crafting these dog-safe cakes goes beyond the ordinary—each recipe is a creative expression of devotion. By using human-grade ingredients, you have the power to ensure your pet enjoys a healthy and delicious indulgence.

These cakes aren't just treats; they're a way to bond with your pup and show them the depth of your affection. Embark on a baking adventure that not only brings joy to your dog but also opens a world of exploration in your kitchen.

Pumpkin and Carrot Cake: A Harvest of Goodness

Indulge your dog's taste buds with this Pumpkin and Carrot Cake, a harmonious blend of whole wheat flour, baking powder, canned pumpkin, grated carrots, honey, and a touch of water and egg. Baked to perfection, this cake is crowned with a sumptuous cream cheese frosting made with plain Greek yogurt. Every slice is a celebration of flavors and textures that your canine companion will adore.

Ingredients
- 1 1/2 cups whole wheat flour
- 1 teaspoon baking powder
- 1/2 cup canned pumpkin
- 1/2 cup grated carrots
- 1/4 cup honey
- 1/4 cup water
- 1 egg

Instructions
1. Preheat oven to 350°F.
2. In a large bowl, mix together the flour and baking powder.
3. In a separate bowl, mix together the pumpkin, carrots, honey, water, and egg.
4. Add the wet ingredients to the dry ingredients and mix until well combined.
5. Pour the batter into a greased 8-inch cake pan.
6. Bake for 25-30 minutes or until a toothpick inserted in the center comes out clean.
7. Let the cake cool completely before frosting with cream cheese frosting made with plain Greek yogurt.

Blueberry and Banana Cake: Bursting with Berry Bliss

For a cake that's as delightful as a summer breeze, try the Blueberry and Banana Cake. Crafted from oat flour, baking powder, fresh blueberries, mashed ripe bananas, honey, and a hint of water and egg, this creation is a fruity symphony. The finishing touch—a cream cheese frosting made with plain Greek yogurt—transforms it into a canine delicacy that's both wholesome and utterly irresistible.

Ingredients
- 2 cups oat flour
- 1 teaspoon baking powder
- 1/2 cup fresh blueberries
- 2 ripe bananas, mashed
- 1/4 cup honey
- 1/4 cup water
- 1 egg

Instructions
1. Preheat oven to 350°F.
2. In a large bowl, mix together the oat flour and baking powder.
3. In a separate bowl, mix together the blueberries, mashed bananas, honey, water, and egg.
4. Add the wet ingredients to the dry ingredients and mix until well combined.
5. Pour the batter into a greased 8-inch cake pan.
6. Bake for 25-30 minutes or until a toothpick inserted in the center comes out clean.
7. Let the cake cool completely before frosting with cream cheese frosting made with plain Greek yogurt.

Sweet Potato and Peanut Butter Cake: A Nutty Delight

Unleash the goodness of this Sweet Potato and Peanut Butter Cake, where whole wheat flour, baking powder, mashed sweet potato, natural peanut butter, honey, and a splash of water and egg come together in perfect harmony. Baked to golden perfection and crowned with a cream cheese frosting made with plain Greek yogurt, this cake promises a medley of flavors that will leave your dog eagerly anticipating every bite.

Ingredients
- 1 1/2 cups whole wheat flour
- 1 teaspoon baking powder
- 1/2 cup mashed sweet potato
- 1/2 cup natural peanut butter
- 1/4 cup honey
- 1/4 cup water
- 1 egg

Instructions
1. Preheat oven to 350°F.
2. In a large bowl, mix together the flour and baking powder.
3. In a separate bowl, mix together the sweet potato, peanut butter, honey, water, and egg.
4. Add the wet ingredients to the dry ingredients and mix until well combined.
5. Pour the batter into a greased 8-inch cake pan.
6. Bake for 25-30 minutes or until a toothpick inserted in the center comes out clean.
7. Let the cake cool completely before frosting with cream cheese frosting made with plain Greek yogurt.

--

Salmon and Brown Rice Cake: A Culinary Delight for Your Canine Companion

Indulge your furry friend in a delightful treat that goes beyond the ordinary with our Salmon and Brown Rice Cake recipe. Crafted with care and precision, this canine-friendly creation promises not just a tasty morsel but a wholesome experience for your beloved pup.

Ingredients
- 1 can of salmon, drained and flaked
- 1 cup cooked brown rice
- 1 cup oat flour
- 2 eggs
- 1 teaspoon baking powder
- 1/4 cup water

Simple Steps for Crafting this Canine Confection:
1. Preheat: Set your oven to 350°F, preparing the stage for the culinary magic ahead.
2. Mix: In a large bowl, combine the salmon, cooked brown rice, oat flour, eggs, baking powder, and water. Ensure a thorough blend for a harmonious texture.
3. Pour: Transfer the mixture into a greased 8-inch cake pan, shaping your culinary creation.
4. Bake: Allow the cake to bake for 25-30 minutes, or until a toothpick inserted in the center comes out clean—a sign of perfection.
5. Cool: Let the cake cool, paving the way for the final touch—a topping of cream cheese frosting made with plain Greek yogurt.

As your canine companion enjoys this delectable creation, you'll witness the tail wags and happy moments that follow. With the Salmon and Brown Rice Cake, you're not just treating your pet; you're offering a nourishing and enjoyable experience that reflects your care and love.

Beef and Potato Cake: A Hearty Delight for Your Pooch

Treat your canine companion to a culinary delight with our Beef and Potato Cake recipe. Crafted with simplicity and care, this wholesome canine-friendly creation promises not just a tasty bite but a fulfilling experience for your four-legged friend.

Ingredients:
- 1 pound ground beef
- 1 cup mashed potatoes
- 1 cup oat flour
- 2 eggs
- 1 teaspoon baking powder
- 1/4 cup water

Simple Steps:
1. Preheat: Set your oven to 350°F, laying the foundation for the culinary creation ahead.
2. Mix: In a large bowl, combine the ground beef, mashed potatoes, oat flour, eggs, baking powder, and water. Ensure a thorough blend for a harmonious texture.
3. Pour: Transfer the mixture into a greased 8-inch cake pan, shaping your culinary creation.
4. Bake: Allow the cake to bake for 25-30 minutes, or until a toothpick inserted in the center comes out clean—a sign of perfection.
5. Cool: Let the cake cool, preparing for the final touch—a topping of cream cheese frosting made with plain Greek yogurt.

As you wrap up this delightful collection of dog-friendly cake recipes, revel in the joy of sharing these special moments with your furry companion. The ritual of crafting these treats and witnessing the anticipation in your pet's eyes adds a layer of joy to the baking experience. Presenting the final creation to your dog, letting them know it's their unique masterpiece, is a heartwarming moment that solidifies the bond between you and your four-legged friend.

And hey, while the savory cakes might not make it to your gourmet palate, rest assured, the sweet ones are people-safe—just in case you're feeling adventurous in sharing a bite of the celebration!

9

RAW FOODS EXAMINED

Exploring the realms of raw food diets for our canine companions is like navigating uncharted waters, filled with both promise and peril. As we embark on this chapter, we find ourselves in the midst of a debate swirling around the benefits and risks associated with feeding dogs raw food. Advocates tout shinier coats, healthier skin, cleaner teeth, and higher energy levels as potential rewards, while caution flags are raised due to potential bacterial contamination, choking hazards, and nutritional imbalances. This intricate landscape demands our attention, as responsible pet owners seek the best for their furry friends. Join us as we unravel the complexities of raw food diets, weighing the benefits against the risks, and navigating the controversial waters with the guidance of veterinary expertise. After all, understanding the nuances of raw food diets is crucial in ensuring the optimal health and well-being of our cherished companions.

Raw food diets for dogs are controversial, and there are both benefits and risks associated with feeding dogs raw food.

Raw food diets for dogs have both benefits and risks. While they may offer some health benefits, they can also pose health risks if not properly formulated. It is important to consult with a veterinarian or a veterinary nutritionist before starting your dog on a raw food diet.

Here are some of the risks and benefits of raw food diets for dogs:

Benefits:
- Shinier coats
- Healthier skin
- Cleaner teeth and better breath
- Higher energy levels
- Smaller stools

Risks:
- Raw meat may contain bacteria and parasites that can lead to infections in dogs.
- Raw diets often contain bones that can cause choking, broken teeth, and damage or obstruction to the digestive tract.
- Raw food could be contaminated and lead to bacterial infections that compromise your dog's health.
- Raw diets have been found to be more likely to contain disease-causing bacteria than commercial pet food.
- Raw diets can be nutritionally unbalanced if not properly formulated.

Advocates of raw food diets for dogs claim that they have numerous health benefits, such as a reduced risk of cancer, dental disease, and allergies. However, there is no reliable scientific evidence to support these claims.

Feeding your dog a raw food diet means taking their nutrition into your own hands. While this can be one of the main appeals of the diet, it can also lead to severe health issues if not properly formulated. It is important to consult with a veterinarian or a veterinary nutritionist before starting your dog on a raw food diet.

Raw food diets for dogs can be nutritionally deficient if not properly formulated.

Here are some common nutrient deficiencies in raw food diets for dogs:

1. Manganese: Raw diets are often low in manganese, which is an essential mineral for dogs. A manganese deficiency can lead to skeletal abnormalities, poor growth, and reproductive failure.

2. Omega-3 Fatty Acids: Many raw diets are deficient in omega-3 fatty acids, which are important for maintaining healthy skin and coat, reducing inflammation, and supporting brain and eye development.

3. Calcium: A calcium deficiency is common in some dogs that eat raw food, which can lead to skeletal abnormalities, poor growth, and dental problems.

4. Iron: Iron is important for the production of red blood cells and oxygen transport in the body. A deficiency in iron can lead to anemia and other health problems.

5. Zinc: Zinc is important for immune function, wound healing, and skin health. A deficiency in zinc can lead to skin problems, poor growth, and immune dysfunction.

6. Vitamins A, D, and E: These vitamins are important for maintaining healthy skin and coat, supporting immune function, and promoting healthy vision. Deficiencies in these vitamins can lead to a range of health problems.

It is important to consult with a veterinarian or a veterinary nutritionist before starting your dog on a raw food diet to ensure that it is nutritionally balanced and safe for your dog to eat.

Raw food can be a healthy addition to a dog's diet, but it is important to know which foods are safe to feed your dog.

Here are some common types of raw food that are safe for dogs to eat:

1. Muscle Meat: Raw muscle meat from chicken, turkey, beef, lamb, and pork is safe for dogs to eat. It is a good source of protein and essential amino acids.

2. Organ Meat: Raw organ meat, such as liver, kidney, and heart, is also safe for dogs to eat. It is a good source of vitamins and minerals.

3. Raw Edible Bones: Raw bones that are soft and edible, such as chicken necks, wings, and backs, are safe for dogs to eat. They are a good source of calcium and other minerals.

4. Fruits and Vegetables: Raw fruits and vegetables, such as apples, carrots, broccoli, and spinach, are safe for dogs to eat. They are a good source of vitamins, minerals, and fiber.

5. Dairy: Some dairy products, such as plain yogurt and cottage cheese, are safe for dogs to eat. They are a good source of protein and calcium.

It is important to note that not all raw foods are safe for dogs to eat. Some raw foods, such as raw eggs, raw fish, and raw pork, can contain harmful bacteria and parasites that can make your dog sick. It is also important to consult with a veterinarian or a veterinary nutritionist before starting your dog on a raw food diet to ensure that it is nutritionally balanced and safe for your dog to eat.

Here are some ways to ensure that a raw food diet is nutritionally balanced for your dog:

1. Feed a variety of proteins: Feeding a variety of proteins, such as chicken, beef, lamb, and fish, can help ensure that your dog is getting a balanced mix of amino acids, vitamins, and minerals.

2. Include organ meat: Organ meat, such as liver and kidney, is a good source of essential nutrients, including vitamins A, D, and K, as well as iron and copper.

3. Add vegetables and fruits: Vegetables and fruits can provide your dog with essential vitamins, minerals, and fiber. Some good options include carrots, sweet potatoes, spinach, and blueberries.

4. Include raw bones: Raw bones can provide your dog with calcium and other minerals. Make sure to choose bones that are appropriate for your dog's size and breed, and supervise your dog while they are eating them.

5. Consult with a veterinarian or veterinary nutritionist: A veterinarian or veterinary nutritionist can help you create a balanced raw food diet that meets your dog's nutritional needs. They can also help you determine the appropriate portion sizes and feeding schedule for your dog.

In conclusion, feeding your dog a raw food diet can be a healthy and nutritious option, but it is important to ensure that the diet is nutritionally balanced. Feeding a variety of proteins, including organ meat, vegetables, and fruits, and consulting with a veterinarian or veterinary nutritionist can help ensure that your dog is getting all the essential nutrients they need.

When feeding a raw food diet to your dog, there are several common mistakes to avoid. Here are some of the most common mistakes to avoid:

1. Incomplete Homework: Not doing enough research before starting your dog on a raw food diet can lead to nutritional imbalances and other health problems.

2. Rushing The Transition: Transitioning your dog to a raw food diet too quickly can cause digestive upset and other health problems. It is important to make the transition gradually over several weeks.

3. Feeding Enhanced Meats: Enhanced meats, such as those that have been injected with sodium or other additives, can be harmful to your dog's health.

4. Not Feeding Bone: Raw bones are an important source of calcium and other minerals for dogs. Not feeding enough bone can lead to nutritional imbalances.

5. Feeding Too Much Bone: Feeding too much bone can lead to constipation, blockages, and other digestive problems.

6. Feeding Unsafe Bones: Some bones, such as cooked bones and bones that are too small or too large, can be dangerous for dogs to eat.

7. Introducing New Foods Too Quickly: **Introducing new foods too quickly can** cause digestive upset and other health problems. It is important to introduce new foods gradually over several weeks.

8. Not Consulting with a Veterinarian: It is important to consult with a veterinarian or a veterinary nutritionist before starting your dog on a raw food diet to ensure that it is nutritionally balanced and safe for your dog to eat.

In conclusion, feeding your dog a raw food diet can be a healthy and nutritious option, but it is important to avoid these common mistakes to ensure that your dog is getting all the essential nutrients they need. Doing your research, transitioning gradually, feeding a balanced diet, and consulting with a veterinarian can help ensure that your dog stays healthy and happy on a raw food diet.

Symptoms of nutrient deficiencies in dogs on a raw food diet can vary depending on the specific nutrient that is lacking. Here are some common symptoms of nutrient deficiencies in dogs on a raw food diet:

1. Poor Growth: A deficiency in essential nutrients, such as calcium, can lead to poor growth in puppies and young dogs.

2. Skeletal Abnormalities: A deficiency in manganese or calcium can lead to skeletal abnormalities, such as bowed legs or a crooked spine.

3. Reproductive Failure: A deficiency in manganese can lead to reproductive failure in dogs.

4. Dull Coat: A deficiency in omega-3 fatty acids can lead to a dull coat and dry, itchy skin.

5. Diarrhea: A deficiency in vitamin B12 can cause diarrhea in dogs.

6. Poor Immunity: A deficiency in essential vitamins and minerals can weaken a dog's immune system, making them more susceptible to infections and illnesses.

7. Anal Gland Problems: A deficiency in fiber can lead to anal gland problems, such as impaction or infection.

8. Flatulence: A diet that is high in fat or poorly balanced can lead to flatulence in dogs.

In conclusion, nutrient deficiencies in dogs on a raw food diet can lead to a range of health problems. It is important to consult with a veterinarian or a veterinary nutritionist before starting your dog on a raw food diet to ensure that it is nutritionally balanced and safe for your dog to eat. If you notice any symptoms of nutrient deficiencies in your dog, it is important to seek veterinary care to address the issue.

You can supplement a raw food diet with vitamins and minerals to prevent nutrient deficiencies in dogs. Here are some common supplements that can be added to a raw food diet for dogs:

1. Essential Fatty Acids: Omega-3 fatty acids, such as fish oil or flaxseed oil, can be added to a raw food diet to support healthy skin and coat, reduce inflammation, and support brain and eye development.

2. Trace Vitamins, Minerals, and Antioxidants: Supplements that contain trace vitamins, minerals, and antioxidants, such as alfalfa, bladder wrack, dandelion, and nettle, can be added to a raw food diet to ensure that your dog is getting all the essential nutrients they need.

3. Calcium and Phosphorus: Supplements that contain calcium and phosphorus, such as bone meal powder, can be added to a raw food diet to support healthy bones and teeth.

4. Probiotics: Probiotics can be added to a raw food diet to support healthy digestion and immune function.

5. Vitamin A, B12, E, and K: Supplements that contain these vitamins can be added to a raw food diet to support healthy vision, skin and coat, immune function, and bone health.

It is important to consult with a veterinarian or a veterinary nutritionist before adding supplements to your dog's raw food diet to ensure that they are getting all the essential nutrients they need. It is also important to choose high-quality supplements that are made from whole foods and are free from harmful additives.

10

OTHER CONSIDERATIONS FOR A HEALTHY DOG LIFESTYLE

Welcome to the final chapter of our culinary journey for your four-legged friend. As we've explored the art of crafting delectable meals and treats, we must now delve into the broader canvas of maintaining a healthy and happy lifestyle for your beloved canine companion. In 'Other Considerations for a Healthy Dog Lifestyle,' we'll unravel key aspects beyond the kitchen that contribute to the overall well-being of your furry friend. From exercise routines and mental stimulation to creating a safe haven at home, let's paint a complete picture of a fulfilling life for your canine companion. So, buckle up as we embark on this holistic exploration to ensure your dog's health and happiness transcend the dining table, making every wag of their tail a testament to a life well-lived.

EXERCISE: HOW MUCH

Right, let's talk about the dog's exercise routine, shall we? It's not a one-size-fits-all situation; we're dealing with a variety of breeds, weights, ages, and activity levels. Small breeds, those little ones under 20 pounds, need a solid 30-60 minutes a day of walks and playtime – keeping them active and engaged.

Now, for the medium-sized fellas in the 21-50 pound range, we're looking at a bit more commitment – 1-2 hours a day, including walks, runs, and playtime. Gotta get that energy out, you know?

Moving on to the big boys, the large breeds weighing in between 51-100 pounds – they're not exempt either. They need that 1-2 hours of daily exercise, walks, runs, and some quality playtime.

Ah, but let's not forget the giants, the ones tipping the scales over 100 pounds. Now, they're the marathon runners of the canine world – a solid 2-3 hours a day of exercise, including walks, runs, and you guessed it, playtime. We're talking about some serious workout sessions here.

However, and I can't stress this enough, these are just guidelines. Each dog is an individual – like us, they have different needs. Factors like age, weight, breed, and how much they zoom around the house can affect their exercise requirements. Oh, and mental stimulation is just as crucial as physical activity – get those brains working with some training, puzzle toys, and interactive play.

But, and this is a big but, always consult with your vet. They're the experts on your dog's health, and they can help tailor the perfect exercise routine. So, no excuses, get those pups moving, keep them engaged, and let's see those tails wagging in happiness!

EXERCISE: ENOUGH?

There are several signs that can indicate whether your dog is getting enough exercise or not. Here are some common signs to look out for:

1. Weight Gain: If your dog is gaining weight or becoming overweight, it may be a sign that they are not getting enough exercise.

2. Destructive Behavior: Dogs that are not getting enough exercise may become bored and engage in destructive behavior, such as chewing on furniture or digging holes in the yard.

3. Restlessness: Dogs that are not getting enough exercise may become restless and have difficulty settling down.

4. Withdrawn or Depressed Behavior: Dogs that are not getting enough exercise may become withdrawn or depressed, and may lose interest in activities they once enjoyed.

5. Hyperactivity: While some dogs may become restless when they are not getting enough exercise, others may become hyperactive and have difficulty calming down.

6. Excessive Barking or Whining: Dogs that are not getting enough exercise may become bored and engage in excessive barking or whining.

7. Pulling on the Leash: Dogs that are not getting enough exercise may become overly excited and pull on the leash during walks.

8. Pestering or Annoying Behavior: Dogs that are not getting enough exercise may become overly needy and pestering, seeking attention from their owners.

There are several signs that can indicate whether your dog is getting enough exercise or not. If you notice any of these signs in your dog, it may be time to increase their exercise routine to keep them happy and healthy. It is important to consult with a veterinarian to determine the optimal exercise routine for your dog based on their individual needs and health status.

EXERCISE: SPECIAL NEEDS

Low-impact exercises can be a great way to keep your dog active and engaged, even if they have limited mobility. Walking, swimming, nose work, learning commands, gentle play sessions, scavenger hunts, and light massage are all great low-impact exercises for dogs with limited mobility. It is important to consult with a veterinarian to determine the optimal exercise routine for your dog based on their individual needs and health status.

Here are some low-impact exercises for dogs with limited mobility:

1. Walking: Slow strolls are an excellent form of low-impact exercise for dogs with limited mobility. Remember, walks should be nice and quiet until your dog heals or gains strength.

2. Swimming: Swimming is another great low-impact activity that you can do with your dog. Not only does it provide a great workout, but it is also a lot of fun!

3. Nose Work: Nose work is a great way to engage your dog's mind and provide them with a low-impact workout. You can hide treats or toys around the house or yard and encourage your dog to find them using their sense of smell.

4. Learning Commands: Teaching your dog new commands can be a great way to provide them with mental stimulation and a low-impact workout. You can teach your dog basic obedience commands, such as sit, stay, and come, or more advanced tricks, such as roll over or play dead.

5. Gentle Play Sessions: Gentle play sessions, such as tug-of-war or fetch, can be a great way to provide your dog with a low-impact workout. Just be sure to choose toys that are appropriate for your dog's size and strength.

6. Scavenger Hunts: Scatter your dog's kibble in the grass and have them search for it. This is a great way to provide your dog with mental stimulation and a low-impact workout.

7. Light Massage: While not as active a form of exercise, light massage is especially helpful for dogs with mobility challenges. With your dog lying prone, you will massage each part of their body, including their legs, back, and neck.

EXERCISE: MENTAL & EMOTIONAL FITNESS

Ensuring your dog's mental fitness and emotional health requires a combination of physical exercise, mental enrichment, a balanced diet, and regular veterinary care. Bonding over fun activities, learning to spot signs of distress, and trying massage and body awareness exercises can also help improve your dog's mental health. By incorporating these strategies into your dog's daily routine, you can help ensure that they are happy, healthy, and thriving.

1. Learn to Spot Signs of Distress: It is important to learn how to spot signs of distress in your dog, such as excessive barking, destructive behavior, and changes in appetite or sleep patterns. This can help you identify potential mental health issues early on and seek appropriate treatment.

2. Exercise Your Dog: Regular exercise is important for both physical and mental health. It can help reduce stress and anxiety, improve mood, and promote better sleep.

3. Provide Mental Enrichment: Mental enrichment activities, such as puzzle toys, interactive games, and training sessions, can help keep your dog's mind active and engaged. This can help reduce boredom and prevent destructive behavior.

4. Try Massage and Body Awareness: Massage and body awareness exercises, such as gentle stretching and massage, can help reduce stress and anxiety in dogs. They can also improve flexibility and mobility, which can help prevent injuries.

5. Give Your Dog a Balanced Diet: A balanced diet that is rich in essential nutrients, such as omega-3 fatty acids and antioxidants, can help support your dog's overall health, including their mental health.

6. Bond Over Fun Activities: Spending quality time with your dog, such as going for walks, playing games, and cuddling, can help strengthen your bond and improve your dog's emotional well-being.

7. Visit the Vet Regularly: Regular visits to the vet can help ensure that your dog is healthy and free from any underlying health issues that may be affecting their mental health.

EXERCISE: PUZZLE TOYS FOR DOGS

Puzzle toys can be a great way to provide mental stimulation and a fun challenge for your dog. Outward Hound Hide N Slide Puzzle Toy, Pet Zone IQ Treat Ball, KONG Classic Dog Toy, Nina Ottosson Dog Tornado Puzzle Toy, Trixie Mad Scientist Puzzle Toy, K9 Connectables, Loobani Dog Feeder Toy, and Outward Hound Wobble Bowl are all great examples of puzzle toys for dogs. It is important to choose toys that are appropriate for your dog's size, strength, and activity level, and to supervise your dog during playtime to ensure their safety.

1. Outward Hound Hide N Slide Puzzle Toy: This puzzle toy features sliding compartments that hide treats or kibble, encouraging your dog to use their problem-solving skills to find the reward.

2. Pet Zone IQ Treat Ball: This ball dispenses treats as your dog plays with it, providing mental stimulation and a fun challenge.

3. KONG Classic Dog Toy: This classic toy can be filled with treats or peanut butter and provides a fun challenge for your dog as they try to get the reward out.

4. Nina Ottosson Dog Tornado Puzzle Toy: This puzzle toy features spinning compartments that hide treats or kibble, encouraging your dog to use their problem-solving skills to find the reward.

5. Trixie Mad Scientist Puzzle Toy: This puzzle toy features beakers and tubes that hide treats or kibble, encouraging your dog to use their problem-solving skills to find the reward.

6. K9 Connectables: This puzzle toy features interlocking pieces that can be filled with treats or kibble, providing a fun challenge for your dog as they try to get the reward out.

7. Loobani Dog Feeder Toy: This puzzle toy features a maze-like design that encourages your dog to use their problem-solving skills to find the reward.

8. Outward Hound Wobble Bowl: This puzzle toy features a wobbling design that makes it difficult for your dog to get the reward out, providing a fun challenge.

EXERCISE: WEEKLY FEEDING & ACTIVITY

Here is a sample daily and weekly feeding and activity schedule for dogs by weight and breed:

Small Breeds (under 20 pounds):
- **Daily Feeding:** 1/2 to 1 cup of high-quality dry dog food, divided into two meals.
- **Daily Exercise:** 30-60 minutes of walking or playtime, divided into two sessions.
- **Weekly Activities:** One training session, one puzzle toy session, and one socialization session.

Medium Breeds (21-50 pounds):
- **Daily Feeding:** 1 to 2 cups of high-quality dry dog food, divided into two meals.
- **Daily Exercise:** 1-2 hours of walking, running, or playtime, divided into two sessions.
- **Weekly Activities:** Two training sessions, one puzzle toy session, and one socialization session.

Large Breeds (51-100 pounds):
- **Daily Feeding:** 2 to 4 cups of high-quality dry dog food, divided into two meals.
- **Daily Exercise:** 1-2 hours of walking, running, or playtime, divided into two sessions.
- **Weekly Activities:** Two training sessions, two puzzle toy sessions, and one socialization session.

Giant Breeds (over 100 pounds):
- **Daily Feeding:** 4 to 8 cups of high-quality dry dog food, divided into two meals.
- **Daily Exercise:** 2-3 hours of walking, running, or playtime, divided into two sessions.
- **Weekly Activities:** Three training sessions, two puzzle toy sessions, and two socialization sessions.

It is important to note that these are general guidelines and that individual dogs may require more or less food and exercise depending on their individual needs. It is also important to consult with a veterinarian to determine the optimal feeding and exercise routine for your dog based on their age, weight, and activity level. Additionally, incorporating weekly activities such as training sessions, puzzle toy sessions, and socialization sessions can help keep your dog mentally fit and emotionally healthy. Finally, it is important to schedule regular veterinary visits for your dog to ensure that they are healthy and free from any underlying health issues that may be affecting their mental and physical well-being.

OVERALL CONSIDERATIONS FOR DOG OWNERS

Dogs are more than just pets; they are loyal companions that bring joy, love, and happiness to our lives. As a dog owner, it is important to ensure that your furry friend is healthy, happy, safe, and a good member of your family. Here are some of the best ways to achieve this:

1. Provide Proper Nutrition: A well-balanced diet is essential for your dog's overall health. Consult with a veterinarian to determine the optimal feeding routine for your dog based on their individual needs and health status. Ensure that your dog's diet includes water, proteins, fats, carbohydrates, minerals, and vitamins.

2. Regular Exercise: Ensuring your dog gets regular exercise is an indispensable component of their overall well-being. This regimen isn't just about physical fitness; it's a key player in maintaining their mental health too. Regular exercise has a multitude of benefits, ranging from stress reduction and anxiety alleviation to mood enhancement and improved sleep patterns.

Now, the exercise prescription isn't a one-size-fits-all affair. It's a customized plan, tailored to suit your dog's unique characteristics. Breed, size, age, and activity level are the key determinants. Smaller breeds might find joy in a brisk 30-minute walk, while larger, more energetic ones could benefit from a longer, more robust routine.

But hold on, don't just take a wild guess at the perfect exercise routine. Consult the experts – your veterinarian. They're not just there for vaccinations and emergencies; they're your go-to resource for crafting an exercise plan that aligns perfectly with your dog's individual needs and health status. So, lace up those walking shoes or grab that frisbee – it's time to keep your furry friend in tip-top shape!

3. Regular Veterinary Visits: Regular visits to the vet can help ensure that your dog is healthy and free from any underlying health issues that may be affecting their mental and physical well-being. It is important to schedule regular veterinary visits for your dog to ensure that they are healthy and free from any underlying health issues that may be affecting their mental and physical well-being.

4. Mental Stimulation: Mental stimulation is a crucial aspect of ensuring your dog's overall well-being and preventing behavioral issues. Dogs, like humans, benefit from mental challenges that keep their minds sharp and engaged. Here's why mental stimulation is important and some activities you can incorporate into your dog's routine:

A. Preventing Boredom: Dogs that experience boredom may develop destructive behaviors as a way to cope. Engaging their minds through mental stimulation activities helps alleviate boredom, keeping them content and less likely to engage in undesirable behaviors.

B. Stress Reduction: Mental stimulation can be a great stress reliever for dogs. When they are mentally engaged, it helps reduce anxiety and stress, contributing to a more relaxed and happy demeanor.

C. Enhancing Problem-Solving Skills: Interactive games and puzzle toys encourage dogs to use their problem-solving skills. Figuring out how to get a treat from a puzzle toy or responding to commands during training sessions challenges their cognitive abilities.

D. Bonding Opportunities: Training sessions and interactive games provide excellent opportunities for bonding between you and your dog. Positive interactions during these activities strengthen the bond of trust and communication between you and your furry friend.

E. Physical Exercise Alone Isn't Enough: While physical exercise is important, mental stimulation complements it by providing a holistic approach to your dog's well-being. A tired mind can be as beneficial as a tired body.

Now, here are some activities you can incorporate into your dog's routine for mental stimulation:

- **Puzzle Toys:** Invest in puzzle toys that dispense treats when manipulated correctly. This stimulates your dog's problem-solving abilities.

- **Interactive Games:** Play games that involve decision-making, such as hide-and-seek or fetch. Use toys that require mental effort.

- **Training Sessions:** Regular training sessions, even for simple commands, engage your dog's mind and reinforce positive behavior.

- **Novel Experiences:** Introduce new environments, scents, and toys to keep your dog curious and mentally stimulated.

Remember that mental stimulation is not a one-size-fits-all concept. Pay attention to your dog's preferences and adjust activities accordingly. A variety of mental challenges will contribute to a happy, well-balanced, and intellectually satisfied canine companion.

5. Socialization: Socialization plays a crucial role in a dog's development, contributing to their ability to interact positively with other dogs and people. This process is instrumental in preventing aggressive behavior and enhancing overall behavior. Engaging your dog in various social experiences, such as visits to the dog park, enrollment in obedience classes, and organizing playdates with other dogs, fosters essential social skills. These interactions create a well-rounded and well-behaved canine companion, promoting a positive and harmonious relationship between your dog and the surrounding environment.

6. Positive Reinforcement Training: Positive reinforcement training is a humane and effective approach to teaching dogs new behaviors and reinforcing desired ones. The core principle of positive reinforcement is to reward your dog for exhibiting the behavior you want, making it more likely for the behavior to be repeated in the future. This method focuses on reinforcing positive actions rather than punishing unwanted behaviors.

Here's how positive reinforcement training typically works:

> **A. Reward-Based System:** Positive reinforcement involves using rewards to encourage and strengthen good behavior. Rewards can include treats, praise, toys, or any positive experience that your dog finds enjoyable.

> **B. Timely Rewards:** Timing is crucial. Rewards should be given immediately after your dog displays the desired behavior. This helps your dog associate the behavior with the reward.

> **C. Consistency is Key:** Consistency is vital in positive reinforcement training. Reinforce good behavior every time it occurs, and be consistent in the cues or commands you use.

> **D. Ignore Unwanted Behavior:** Instead of punishing unwanted behavior, positive reinforcement focuses on ignoring or redirecting it. Reinforcing only the behaviors you want helps your dog understand what you expect from them.

> **E. Use Clear Cues:** Clearly communicate the cues for the desired behavior. Dogs respond well to consistent and clear signals, making it easier for them to understand what is expected.

> **F. Patience and Persistence:** Training takes time, especially with complex behaviors. Be patient, stay positive, and persist in reinforcing good behavior.

G. Diverse Rewards: Mix up the types of rewards you use to keep your dog engaged and motivated. Some dogs may be more motivated by treats, while others respond better to praise or play.

Positive reinforcement training not only teaches your dog commands but also builds a strong bond between you and your furry companion. It promotes a positive and enjoyable learning experience, making training sessions something your dog looks forward to. Always tailor your approach to your dog's personality and preferences for the best results. If you're new to dog training, consider seeking guidance from professional trainers who specialize in positive reinforcement techniques.

7. Provide a Safe Environment: Ensuring a safe environment for your dog involves several crucial steps. First and foremost, keeping hazardous items out of reach is essential. This includes securing chemicals, toxic plants, and certain foods to prevent accidental ingestion. Yard safety is another key aspect, requiring a securely fenced area and the removal of potential hazards like toxic plants and gardening tools. Providing a comfortable sleeping area is vital for your dog's overall well-being. Additionally, offering safe chew toys, supervising interactions with children and other pets, securing loose wires, scheduling regular veterinary check-ups, and ensuring proper identification through a collar with ID contribute to creating a secure and happy living space for your canine companion.

In conclusion, ensuring that your dog is healthy, happy, safe, and a good member of your family requires a combination of proper nutrition, regular exercise, mental stimulation, regular veterinary visits, socialization, positive reinforcement training, and a safe environment. By incorporating these strategies into your dog's daily routine, you can help ensure that they are happy, healthy, and thriving. Remember, dogs are more than just pets; they are loyal companions that bring joy, love, and happiness to our lives.

11

The Last Bite: Our Gourmet Canine Feast

Ladies and gentlemen, today I present to you the *pièce de résistance*, the Gourmet Canine Feast: a culinary symphony for your discerning pooch. Now, this isn't your run-of-the-mill kibble; we're talking about a gourmet experience that will make your dog's taste buds sing and dance.

Firstly, let's talk ingredients. We've got prime ground beef – none of that average stuff. We're talking about the Ferrari of meats. Then, quinoa, the ancient grain that's been a staple for centuries, cooked to absolute perfection. Sweet potatoes, hand-mashed for that touch of decadence. Blueberries, individually chosen for quality, because your dog deserves the best. And kale, finely shredded for that pop of color and nutrients.

Now, the eggs – free-range, of course, because we believe in giving your pooch the freedom to enjoy the best. And let's not forget the coconut oil – a touch of the tropics, because your dog deserves a taste of paradise.

But what elevates this dish to culinary greatness is the pinch of turmeric. Not just for the color, but for the anti-inflammatory power it brings to the table. A dash of gold for your canine royalty.

Now, the preparation. We're not just mixing ingredients; we're conducting a culinary symphony. Every element has its part, every note building up to a crescendo of flavor.

And into the oven it goes, baking to perfection. The result? A masterpiece. A canine opus that deserves a standing ovation from your furry friend.

Serve this Gourmet Canine Feast with the love and care your dog deserves. Watch as their eyes light up, their tails wag in approval, and you become the maestro of their culinary world.

This isn't just a meal; it's a gourmet experience crafted for your beloved companion. So, treat your dog to the best – because, in the end, they're not just pets; they're family.

Ingredients:

- 1 pound prime ground beef
- 1 cup quinoa, cooked to perfection
- 1/2 cup sweet potatoes, finely mashed
- 1/4 cup blueberries, handpicked for quality
- 1/4 cup kale, finely shredded
- 2 eggs, free-range and full of flavor
- 1 tablespoon coconut oil, a touch of tropical luxury
- A pinch of turmeric for a dash of golden goodness

Instructions:

1. Preheat your culinary arena to a sizzling 375°F.

2. In a grand mixing bowl, unite the prime ground beef, flawless quinoa, sumptuous sweet potatoes, and the jewels of blueberries. Sprinkle in the finely shredded kale for a burst of color and vibrancy.

3. Crack open the eggs, releasing their golden potential, and let them bind this symphony of flavors together. Don't forget the coconut oil – a tropical maestro conducting the ensemble.

4. Sprinkle a pinch of turmeric, not just for a burst of color but for its anti-inflammatory prowess. A touch of gold for your canine connoisseur.

5. With the precision of a master chef, mix this melange until every note harmonizes, forming a culinary crescendo of aroma and texture.

6. Transfer this opulent creation to a baking pan, shaping it into a masterpiece that echoes your devotion.

7. Into the preheated arena it goes, baking for 25-30 minutes or until the stage is set, and the top is adorned with a hint of golden brown.

8. Let the masterpiece cool, then present it to your four-legged aficionado, whose eager eyes reflect gratitude for this culinary opus.

This Gourmet Canine Feast isn't just a meal; it's a culinary symphony, a crescendo of flavors orchestrated to honor your beloved companion. Serve with love, and watch as tails wag in a standing ovation for your culinary prowess.

12 A LIST OF RECIPES AND RELATED INGREDIENTS

13 Fruitful Guidelines: A Dog Owner's Guide to Canine-Friendly Fruits

In crafting the recipes for this book, the focus was primarily on creating savory and nutritionally balanced meals for dogs. While fruits can be a delightful addition to a dog's diet, it's essential to ensure that the recipes are well-rounded and meet the dietary needs of our canine companions. The appendix at the end of the book provides a comprehensive guide to dog-safe fruits and those that should be avoided. This thoughtful inclusion allows dog owners to explore additional treat options for their furry friends and reinforces the importance of responsible and informed pet nutrition. While the main recipes may not heavily feature fruits, the appendix ensures that readers have a handy reference for incorporating these wholesome snacks into their dog's diet. After all, a well-fed and happy dog is the ultimate goal!

Dog-Safe Fruits:
1. Apples (without seeds and core)
2. Blueberries
3. Strawberries
4. Watermelon (seedless and without rind)
5. Bananas
6. Pineapple
7. Mango (without pit)
8. Oranges (in moderation)
9. Cranberries (fresh or dried)
10. Peaches (without pit)

Fruits Not Safe for Dogs:
1. Grapes and raisins (toxic and can cause kidney failure)
2. Cherries (pits and stems contain cyanide)
3. Citrus fruits in large amounts (can cause upset stomach)
4. Persimmons (can cause intestinal blockages)
5. Stone fruits with pits (peaches, plums, apricots)
6. UnProcessed Avocado (contains persin, which is toxic to dogs)
7. Rhubarb (leaves are toxic)
8. Unripe tomatoes (contain solanine, which can be harmful)
9. Fruit pits and seeds (can be a choking hazard)
10. Fruit with added sugars or artificial sweeteners (like xylitol)

Our Dog-Friendly Fruit Recipe:

Frozen Fruit Dog Treats

Ingredients:
- 1 cup blueberries
- 1 cup strawberries (hulled and sliced)
- 1 cup plain yogurt (no added sugars)
- 1 tablespoon honey (optional)

Instructions:
1. Blend the blueberries, strawberries, yogurt, and honey in a blender until smooth.
2. Pour the mixture into ice cube trays or silicone molds.
3. Freeze for a few hours or until solid.
4. Pop out the frozen treats and let your dog enjoy this refreshing snack.

14 FINAL THOUGHTS

In the journey through the pages of this comprehensive guide on dog culinary options, nutrition, and homemade treats, one cannot help but be stirred by the immense impact we can have on our canine companions' lives. As we delve into the intricacies of preparing wholesome meals for our dogs, we not only unlock the key to their physical well-being but also embark on a culinary adventure that adds an element of joy to their daily lives.

The exploration of nutritious recipes becomes a shared experience, creating a unique bond between dog and owner. From the delectable Salmon and Brown Rice Cake to the heartwarming Sweet Potato and Peanut Butter Cake, each recipe is crafted not just to satisfy canine taste buds but also to ignite a sense of culinary creativity in their human companions.

As we navigate the intricacies of dog health, from exercise routines to mental stimulation, it becomes evident that our furry friends are more than just companions—they are teachers. The commitment to their well-being mirrors our capacity for empathy, responsibility, and compassion. Through the lens of their unyielding loyalty, dogs impart profound lessons on how to be better humans.

In the culmination of this insightful journey, the value of dogs as pets resonates beyond the realm of companionship. They become catalysts for personal growth, teaching us to be much better than we expected we could be.

www.ingramcontent.com/pod-product-compliance
Lightning Source LLC
Chambersburg PA
CBHW051309120626
46547CB00015B/2152